Reading With Ease: An Alternative Method - Volume 3

By

Elaine M. Peters. MSc. Ed.

Copyright

ISBN: 978-1-969978-96-8

Dedication

To my daughter, whose perseverance and kind heart continues to inspire me.

To my husband and my son, who have provided the unwavering support I've needed to complete this book.

About the Author

Elaine Marsha Peters, born 1956 in Toronto, Ontario, Canada, earned an Honors B.A. in Physical Health Education, followed later in life with a Master of Science in Education. Since 1993, Elaine has been a strong advocate and teacher for children, youth, and adults who learn differently. She served as Chair on Parent-Teacher counsels, co-founded a charitable non-profit organization committed to enhancing the lives of adolescents and adults with developmental disabilities through social inclusion, and most recently, has written procedural guides for improving the reading skills of non-readers using research-based alternative methods she developed during her Master of Science in Education practicum.

Contents

Copyright *ii*
Dedication *iii*
About the Author *iv*
Synopsis *vii*
Foreword *viii*
References *xiii*
Pre-Teaching Vocabulary *xv*
Story 1 **1**
Story 2 **9**
Story 3 **17**
Story 4 **25**
Story 5 **33**
Story 6 **41**
Story 7 **49**
Story 8 **57**
Story 9 **65**
Story 10 **73**
Story 11 **81**
Story 12 **89**
Story 13 **97**
Story 14 **105**
Story 15 **113**
Story 16 **121**
Story 17 **129**
Story 18 **137**

Story 19 **145**
Story 20 **153**
Spelling Made Fun! **161**
Sentence Building (Mirroring) **164**
Sentence Building (Freestyle) **166**
Inferencing Skill Building **167**
Parts of Speech: Classifying Words as Nouns and Pronouns **168**
Appendix: Master Word List Data Sheet **170**
Afterword **176**

Synopsis

As a concerned and deeply engaged parent of a child with moderately severe autism and an intellectual disability, discovering there was a vast gap in the quality of education available for our daughter was challenging. The positive aspect of the challenges we faced advocating for education curriculum, instruction, and assessment equality, is this (and future) series of An Alternative Method for beginner readers. Creating an alternative reader series was a labor of love. Coalescing decades of literacy research such as pre-teaching vocabulary sight words combined with the processes of teaching phonetics paired with word symbols, I created a learning strategy that helped our daughter and others improve their reading skills. Not only did she learn to read but she also developed a desire to continue her own lifelong learning journey into the wonders of written language. This third of seven learning-to-read procedural guides opens the door to the discovery of written language for children, youth, and adults who are unique learners.

Foreword

Further to the foreword's of Reading with Ease: An Alternative Method, book volumes 1 and 2, I provide more research evidence regarding the use of reading strategies for improving, specifically, reading comprehension.

Reading comprehension is the ability of a reader to develop or create contextual meaning from written language. Developing reading comprehension is a complex task. The complexity necessitates plentiful practice and fading instructional support over time (i.e., scaffolded instruction) about decoding words, creating cognitively sound understandings about the meaning of each word as well as the contextual meaning of each sentence read and how they all interconnect to tell a story with a main idea. Duke and Pearson (2002) describe reading comprehension as "an active, cognitive process. This process includes the construction, revision, and continuous questioning of the meanings a reader makes while engaged in the active reading of written text."

Peer reviewed research studies reveal that the critical predictors of effective reading comprehension were one's phonological knowledge of letters plus the ability to decode words in text and understand the meaning of words (i.e., create a mental representation of each word). Decoding words refers to the process of quickly identifying a letter or combination of letters to their sounds, thus distinguishing the patterns that make consonants, syllables, and consequently, words.

Evolution in the development of reading comprehension gradually becomes increasingly supported by one's skills in oral language. These skills include the extent of one's vocabulary, ability to remember a story's details, as well as the ability to keep track of word order and relationships between words in phrases and/or sentences, which is known as syntactic knowledge (Johnston, Barnes, and Desrochers, 2008). Research by Kim and Petscher (2023) as well as Dujardin, Ecalle, Auphan, Bailloud, and Magnan (2023) support the importance of developing vocabulary knowledge. Kim and Petscher (2023) found that "individuals with reading comprehension difficulties have low vocabulary knowledge". As well, Dujardin, Ecalle, Auphan, Bailloud, and Magnan (2023) discovered that "word reading plays a central role in reading comprehension and is underpinned by the influence of vocabulary" where vocabulary depth and word reading were dependent on one's ability to know the phonetic pronunciation of words, the correct spelling of words, and each word's meaning.

Other studies found that improving inferencing skills (that is, critical thinking skills) also increased reading comprehension skills. Improving inferencing skills using a reading coach who uses scaffolded intent through leading dialogue that focus on who, what, where, when, why, and how. Scaffolded intent refers to the method of splitting instruction into small units with the reading coach decreasing their support as the reader learns new reading skills.

For example, using Reading with Ease: An Alternative Method volume 3's story number 8: Who benefits from looking after living things on this world?; What can each person do to help look after living things on this world?; Where in the world is the biggest problem stopping people from looking after living things on this world?; When is the best time to act on looking after living things on this world?; Why should people know about the importance of looking after living things on this world?; and, How does looking after living things on this world help us and other people? Over time, the reading coach reduces their direct questioning of the reader about a story's who, what, where, when, why, and how. Since research indicates that inferences involve connecting prior knowledge with the text a person reads, it is reasonable to propose the use of videos and in person environmental observational learning facilities (such as Field Centers, etc.) focused on ecological conservation are valuable resources for deepening understanding and knowledge about the importance for human stewardship regarding living things with whom we share this planet.

Additionally, in their chapter on Reading Comprehension, Ferlazzo and Sypnieski (2018) state, "Recent research on the explicit teaching of prosody [i.e., inflection] to students indicates it can improve fluency skills and reading comprehension. Reading comprehension researchers have found that explicit instruction in reading strategies can benefit comprehension.

[The use of] Reading [coaches assisting beginner readers to read] the text [enabling] them to model pronunciation and prosody and frees students to focus on comprehension" Ferlazzo and Sypnieski (2018). Reading with Ease: An Alternative Method follows these precepts using a structured, scaffolded intent approach.

Johnston, Barnes, and Desrochers (2008) cite research studies that provide deeper understanding about reading comprehension. For example, they mention research studies that found working memory and the ability to control one's focus (an executive function of the brain), are important cognitive resources required for the successful amalgamation of unfamiliar words, phrases, and/or sentences. More precisely, "working memory serves as a mental workspace where information retrieved from memory (either world knowledge or previously read text) is available for integration with incoming text or contributes to updating and revision of the mental representation of the unfolding text or discourse" (Johnston, Barnes, and Desrochers, 2008). Therefore, if working memory resources are insufficient or easily overloaded, or if one's ability to control one's focus are underdeveloped, the successful amalgamation of words, phrases, and/or sentences will falter. Hence, Johnston, Barnes, and Desrochers (2008) cite research studies that posit that instructional strategies assist to strengthen underdeveloped comprehending skills by reducing the "demands on working memory". The Reading with Ease: An Alternative Method series provides a clear, well-organised, procedural instructional strategy approach with teacher/parent/peer coach modeling.

Thus, the procedural strategies provided in the Reading with Ease: An Alternative Method series will assist to strengthen reading comprehension by building the fundamental skills required for the successful amalgamation of one's world knowledge, text previously read, and mental representation.

Furthermore, Johnston, Barnes, and Desrochers (2008) state that "Narratives are the most common genre for prereaders, [as they] are particularly suited to provide a bridge between oral language and text comprehension." The Reading with Ease: An Alternative Method series, provides twenty short narratives per book volume, thus satisfying this bridging necessity.

In conclusion, the evidence collected from peer reviewed research studies conducted over many years support the premise that, "The most effective interventions for children [youth, or adults] with comprehension problems are those that provide explicit instruction in areas of deficit (e.g., vocabulary) or in those skills critical for the development of skilled comprehension—strategies that work together to enhance inferential skills and new learning from text" Johnston, Barnes, and Desrochers (2008). The Reading with Ease: An Alternative Method series fulfills these criteria through its easy-to-follow procedural strategies.

References

- Dujardin, E., Ecalle, J., Auphan, P., Bailloud, N., Magnan, A., (2023). Vocabulary and reading comprehension: what are the links in 7- to 10 - year-old children? Psychology Early, First published: 05 March 2023.

- Duke N.K., and Pearson, P.D., (2002). Effective Practices for Developing Reading Comprehension.Copyright 2002 International Reading Association, Inc

- Ferlazzo, L., & Sypnieski, K.H., (2018). The ELL Teacher's Toolbox: Hundreds of Practical Ideas to Support Your Students, First Edition, Jossey-Bass, A Wiley Brand, First published: 16 April 2018.

- Johnston, A. M., Barnes, M. A., & Desrochers, A. (2008). Reading comprehension: Developmental processes, individual differences, and interventions. Canadian Psychology / Psychologie canadienne, 49(2), 125–132. https://doi.org/10.1037/0708-5591.49.2.125

- Kim, Y.S.G., & Petscher, Y., (2023). Do Spelling and Vocabulary Improve Classification Accuracy of Children's Reading Difficulties Over and Above Word Reading? Reading Research Quarterly, Volume 58, Issue 2, First published: 07 March 2023.

Pre-Teaching Vocabulary

1. Review with the learner the first page of illustrated words presented before each story. If possible, print the page of illustrated words for each story.

2. Cut out and (if possible) laminate each illustrated word block making sure there are smooth round corners, no sharp corners for safety reasons, on the word blocks. Another option is to print each page of illustrated words onto large label sheets (8.5” x 11”). Then, lay the label sheet of word symbol blocks onto a cardboard sheet (8.5” x 11”), which can be cut from an empty cereal box. Next, cut out each word symbol block making sure to round out the corners, again for safety reasons.

3. Have the learner choose a word block.

4. The facilitator says the word aloud, slowly, three times, using a pencil or crayon to point to consonant/vowel of a word while making the sound of that consonant/vowel (phonemes). Then, blend the consonant/vowel sounds (phonemes) to say the word.

5. The facilitator says to the learner, “Your turn.”

6. The facilitator assists with pronunciation as needed. Tapping out the cadence of the word's letter sounds is also helpful.

7. Act out or role-play to express an action word's meaning. Be creative. Try various ways to elicit positive engagement from the learner. Try using a favorite object/video clip of the learner to act out and make clear a word's meaning.

8. Repeat steps 3 to 7 for all ten words. **IMPORTANT**: Provide the learner with a meaningful reward paired with verbal (or signing) "great reading" acknowledgment each time the learner reads a word block accurately. Examples of rewards: verbal or gestural praise such as high fives, smiles, nods, and thumbs ups, or concrete rewards such as favorite stickers, a certain number of minutes playing a video game or watching a video, extra computer time, listening to a favorite riff or song.

9. Lay out 3-word blocks at one time face down. The learner selects one at random, saying the word aloud with help from the facilitator, as necessary. (Modification: If the learner is non-verbal, leave the 3-word blocks face up, the facilitator says a word aloud and the learner points to the word block that represents the word spoken by the facilitator. If correctly identified, turn the word block face down. Continue this process until all the word blocks are face down.)

10. Lay out the next 3-word blocks face down. Follow step 9 instructions.

11. Lay out the remaining 4-word blocks face down. Follow step 9 instructions.

12. Lay out all the 10-word blocks face down. The learner selects one at random, saying the word aloud with help from the facilitator, as necessary. (Modification: If the learner is non-verbal. leave the 10-word blocks face up, the facilitator says a word aloud and the learner points to the word block that represents the word spoken by the facilitator. If correctly identified, turn the word block face down. Continue this process until all the word blocks are face down.)

It is important to remember that positive reinforcement given immediately following the desired behavior (reading the word) increases the likelihood that the behavior will reoccur. Therefore, provide the learner with a meaningful reward (i.e., meaningful to the learner) paired with verbal praise or signing "Great reading" each time the learner accurately reads a word block. Examples of rewards include verbal or gestural praise, such as high-fives, smiles, nods, or thumbs-ups, as well as concrete rewards like favorite stickers, a certain number of minutes playing a video game or watching a video, extra computer time, or listening to a favorite riff or song.

Consistently delivering the positive reinforcement every time the behavior (reading a word block) occurs is IMPORTANT!

Story 1

holding
bowl
where
put
Should eat?
Skip it?
may
eat
then
other
hoping
kindness

Tips for the Reading Facilitator:

Using a sheet of paper, cover all lines/sentences below the line/sentence the learner will read. Once the learner has read the line/sentence (with assistance or independently), uncover the next line/sentence. This technique offers less distraction and more focused attention on the line/sentence to be read.

After the learner reads each line/sentence (with or without assistance), provide positive reinforcement that is meaningful to the learner.
Be creative, use objects or video clips to help exemplify the words being learned.

Use the *Word List Data Sheet* that follows this story to track a learner's progress.

Use the *Master Word List Data Sheet* in the Appendix to track word recognition mastery.

Note: Words appearing in previous stories are regarded as being familiar to the learner. However, some review may be necessary to maintain word recognition and understanding.

The story with word symbols begins on the next page.

I saw you holding a big bowl of

rice today. Where did you put the

rice? My brother may want to eat

some. Then, my other brother may

want to eat some.

I am hoping for your kindness to

let them eat the rice.

Please and thank you!

Tips for the Reading Facilitator:

Once the learner can fluently read the story with word symbols, have them read the same story shown on the next page which eliminates individual word symbols.

Using a sheet of paper, cover all lines/sentences below the line/sentence the learner will read. Once the learner has read the line/sentence (with assistance or independently), uncover the next line/sentence. This technique offers less distraction and more focused attention on the line/sentence to be read.

After the learner reads each line/sentence (with or without assistance), provide positive reinforcement that is meaningful to the learner.

Be creative, use objects or video clips to help exemplify the words being learned.

Use the *Word List Data Sheet* that follows this story to track a learner's progress.

Use the *Master Word List Data Sheet* in the Appendix to track word recognition mastery.

Note: Words appearing in previous stories are regarded as being familiar to the learner. However, some review may be necessary to maintain word recognition and understanding.

I saw you holding a big bowl of rice yesterday. Where did you put the rice? My brother may want to eat some. Then, my other brother may also want to eat some. I am hoping for your kindness to let them eat the rice. Please and thank you!

Word List Data Sheets

(Copy this sheet as often as necessary to track progress over time)

Story 1 Words	Date:			Date:			Date:			Date:			The Date a Word is Mastered
	Assistance	Some Assistance	No Assistance	Assistance	Some Assistance	No Assistance	Assistance	Some Assistance	No Assistance	Assistance	Some Assistance	No Assistance	
holding													
bowl													
where													
put													
may													
eat													
then													
other													
hoping													
kindness													

Story 2

rabbit
still
goes
bed
were
Sun
Mon
Tue
Wed
Thu
Fri
Sat
days
goodbye
animal
different
John
name

Tips for the Reading Facilitator:

Using a sheet of paper, cover all lines/sentences below the line/sentence the learner will read. Once the learner has read the line/sentence (with assistance or independently), uncover the next line/sentence. This technique offers less distraction and more focused attention on the line/sentence to be read.

After the learner reads each line/sentence (with or without assistance), provide positive reinforcement that is meaningful to the learner.
Be creative, use objects or video clips to help exemplify the words being learned.

Use the *Word List Data Sheet* that follows this story to track a learner's progress.

Use the *Master Word List Data Sheet* in the Appendix to track word recognition mastery.

Note: Words appearing in previous stories are regarded as being familiar to the learner. However, some review may be necessary to maintain word recognition and understanding.

The story with word symbols begins on the next page.

My sister has a rabbit. She still

goes to bed with her rabbit.

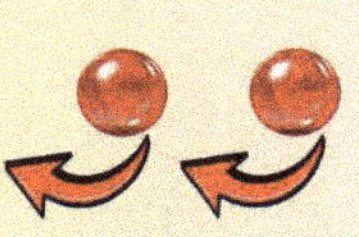 

There were days my sister could

 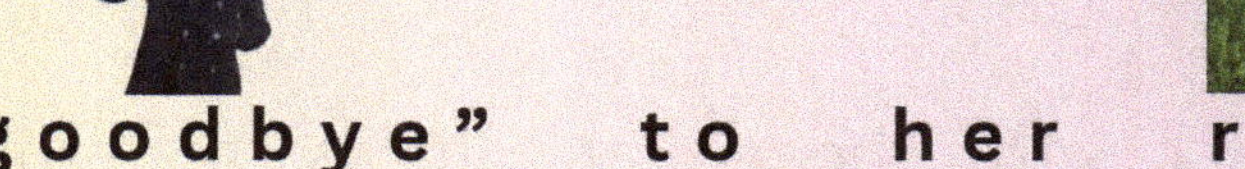

not say "goodbye" to her rabbit

when she had to go out. Her love for

this animal is different than her

love for the other animal she has.

She gave rabbit the name, "Mouse".

Tips for the Reading Facilitator:

Once the learner can fluently read the story with word symbols, have them read the same story shown on the next page which eliminates individual word symbols.

Using a sheet of paper, cover all lines/sentences below the line/sentence the learner will read. Once the learner has read the line/sentence (with assistance or independently), uncover the next line/sentence. This technique offers less distraction and more focused attention on the line/sentence to be read.

After the learner reads each line/sentence (with or without assistance), provide positive reinforcement that is meaningful to the learner.

Be creative, use objects or video clips to help exemplify the words being learned.

Use the *Word List Data Sheet* that follows this story to track a learner's progress.

Use the *Master Word List Data Sheet* in the Appendix to track word recognition mastery.

Note: Words appearing in previous stories are regarded as being familiar to the learner. However, some review may be necessary to maintain word recognition and understanding.

My sister has a rabbit. She still goes to bed with her rabbit.

There were days my sister could not say “goodbye” to her rabbit when she had to go out.

Her love for this animal is different than her love for the other animal she has. She gave her rabbit the name, “Mouse”.

Word List Data Sheets

(Copy this sheet as often as necessary to track progress over time)

Story 2 Words	Date:			Date:			Date:			Date:			The Date a Word is Mastered
	Assistance	Some Assistance	No Assistanc e	Assistance	Some Assistance	No Assistance	Assistance	Some Assistance	No Assistance	Assistance	Some Assistance	No Assistance	
rabbit													
still													
goes													
bed													
were													
days													
goodbye													
animal													
different													
name													

Story 3

paper
page
letter
birthday
party
happen
next
MON
TUE
WED
THU
FRI
SAT
SUN
week
place
means

Tips for the Reading Facilitator:

Using a sheet of paper, cover all lines/sentences below the line/sentence the learner will read. Once the learner has read the line/sentence (with assistance or independently), uncover the next line/sentence. This technique offers less distraction and more focused attention on the line/sentence to be read.

After the learner reads each line/sentence (with or without assistance), provide positive reinforcement that is meaningful to the learner.
Be creative, use objects or video clips to help exemplify the words being learned.

Use the *Word List Data Sheet* that follows this story to track a learner's progress.

Use the *Master Word List Data Sheet* in the Appendix to track word recognition mastery.

Note: Words appearing in previous stories are regarded as being familiar to the learner. However, some review may be necessary to maintain word recognition and understanding.

The story with word symbols begins on the next page.

I must find some paper on which

to write a one page letter to my

friend about the birthday party that

will happen next week. The place

where the birthday party will

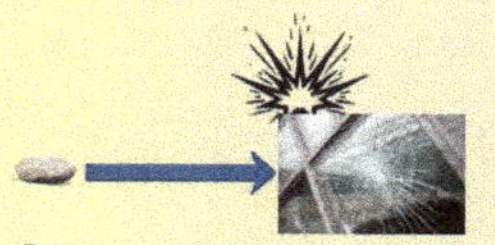

happen is my home.

My friend saying, “Yes, I will be

there”, means so much to me.

Tips for the Reading Facilitator:

Once the learner can fluently read the story with word symbols, have them read the same story shown on the next page which eliminates individual word symbols.

Using a sheet of paper, cover all lines/sentences below the line/sentence the learner will read. Once the learner has read the line/sentence (with assistance or independently), uncover the next line/sentence. This technique offers less distraction and more focused attention on the line/sentence to be read.

After the learner reads each line/sentence (with or without assistance), provide positive reinforcement that is meaningful to the learner.

Be creative, use objects or video clips to help exemplify the words being learned.

Use the *Word List Data Sheet* that follows this story to track a learner's progress.

Use the *Master Word List Data Sheet* in the Appendix to track word recognition mastery.

Note: Words appearing in previous stories are regarded as being familiar to the learner. However, some review may be necessary to maintain word recognition and understanding.

I must find some paper on which to write a letter to my friend about the birthday party that will happen next week. The place where the birthday party will happen is my home.

My friend saying, “Yes, I will be there”, means so much to me.

Sun	Mon	Tue	Wed	Thu	Fri	Sat
1	2	3	4	5	6	7
8	9	10	11	12	13	14
15	16	17	18	19	20	21
22	23	24	25	26	27	28
29	30	31				

Word List Data Sheets

(Copy this sheet as often as necessary to track progress over time)

Story 3 Words	Date:			Date:			Date:			Date:			The Date a Word is Mastered
	Assistance	Some Assistance	No Assistance	Assistance	Some Assistance	No Assistance	Assistance	Some Assistance	No Assistance	Assistance	Some Assistance	No Assistance	
paper													
page													
letter													
birthday													
party													
happen													
next													
week													
place													
means													

Story 4

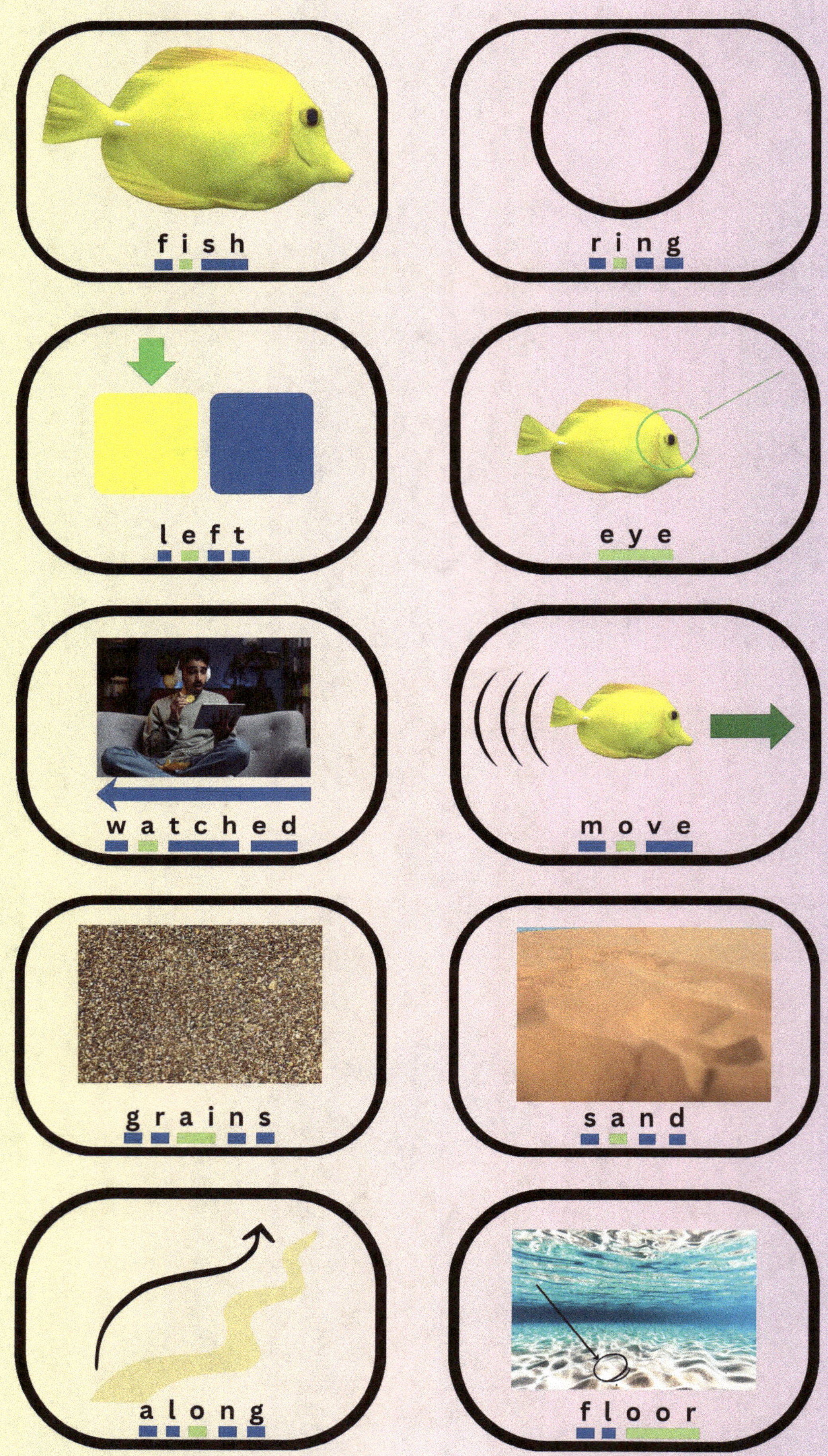
fish
ring
left
eye
watched
move
grains
sand
along
floor

Tips for the Reading Facilitator:

Using a sheet of paper, cover all lines/sentences below the line/sentence the learner will read. Once the learner has read the line/sentence (with assistance or independently), uncover the next line/sentence. This technique offers less distraction and more focused attention on the line/sentence to be read.

After the learner reads each line/sentence (with or without assistance), provide positive reinforcement that is meaningful to the learner.
Be creative, use objects or video clips to help exemplify the words being learned.

Use the *Word List Data Sheet* that follows this story to track a learner's progress.

Use the *Master Word List Data Sheet* in the Appendix to track word recognition mastery.

Note: Words appearing in previous stories are regarded as being familiar to the learner. However, some review may be necessary to maintain word recognition and understanding.

The story with word symbols begins on the next page.

I saw a pretty yellow fish with a

black ring along its left eye.

I watched the fish move the

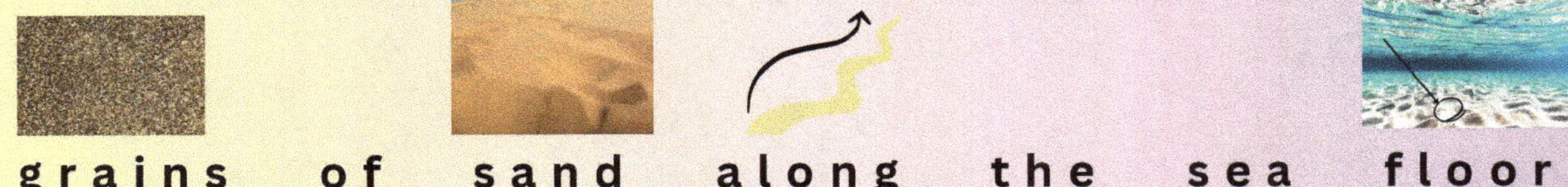

grains of sand along the sea floor.

Tips for the Reading Facilitator:

Once the learner can fluently read the story with word symbols, have them read the same story shown on the next page which eliminates individual word symbols.

Using a sheet of paper, cover all lines/sentences below the line/sentence the learner will read. Once the learner has read the line/sentence (with assistance or independently), uncover the next line/sentence. This technique offers less distraction and more focused attention on the line/sentence to be read.

After the learner reads each line/sentence (with or without assistance), provide positive reinforcement that is meaningful to the learner.

Be creative, use objects or video clips to help exemplify the words being learned.

Use the *Word List Data Sheet* that follows this story to track a learner's progress.

Use the *Master Word List Data Sheet* in the Appendix to track word recognition mastery.

Note: Words appearing in previous stories are regarded as being familiar to the learner. However, some review may be necessary to maintain word recognition and understanding.

I saw a pretty yellow fish with a black ring around its left eye.

I watched the fish move the grains of sand along the sea floor.

Word List Data Sheets

(Copy this sheet as often as necessary to track progress over time)

Story 4 Words	Date:			Date:			Date:			Date:			The Date a Word is Mastered
	Assistance	Some Assistance	No Assistance	Assistance	Some Assistance	No Assistance	Assistance	Some Assistance	No Assistance	Assistance	Some Assistance	No Assistance	
fish													
ring													
left													
eye													
watched													
move													
grains													
sand													
along													
floor													

Story 5

pet
chameleon
change
color
end
tail
large
follow
bedroom
beautiful

Tips for the Reading Facilitator:

Using a sheet of paper, cover all lines/sentences below the line/sentence the learner will read. Once the learner has read the line/sentence (with assistance or independently), uncover the next line/sentence. This technique offers less distraction and more focused attention on the line/sentence to be read.

After the learner reads each line/sentence (with or without assistance), provide positive reinforcement that is meaningful to the learner.
Be creative, use objects or video clips to help exemplify the words being learned.

Use the *Word List Data Sheet* that follows this story to track a learner's progress.

Use the *Master Word List Data Sheet* in the Appendix to track word recognition mastery.

Note: Words appearing in previous stories are regarded as being familiar to the learner. However, some review may be necessary to maintain word recognition and understanding.

The story with word symbols begins on the next page.

My pet chameleon can change its

color from its nose to the end

of its tail. My pet chameleon is

not large. I follow him around my

bedroom. He is a very beautiful

chameleon.

Tips for the Reading Facilitator:

Once the learner can fluently read the story with word symbols, have them read the same story shown on the next page which eliminates individual word symbols.

Using a sheet of paper, cover all lines/sentences below the line/sentence the learner will read. Once the learner has read the line/sentence (with assistance or independently), uncover the next line/sentence. This technique offers less distraction and more focused attention on the line/sentence to be read.

After the learner reads each line/sentence (with or without assistance), provide positive reinforcement that is meaningful to the learner.

Be creative, use objects or video clips to help exemplify the words being learned.

Use the *Word List Data Sheet* that follows this story to track a learner's progress.

Use the *Master Word List Data Sheet* in the Appendix to track word recognition mastery.

Note: Words appearing in previous stories are regarded as being familiar to the learner. However, some review may be necessary to maintain word recognition and understanding.

My pet chameleon can change its color from its nose to the end of its tail. My pet chameleon is not large. I follow him around my bedroom. He is a very beautiful chameleon.

Word List Data Sheets

(Copy this sheet as often as necessary to track progress over time)

Story 5 Words	Date:			Date:			Date:			Date:			The Date a Word is Mastered
	Assistance	Some Assistance	No Assistance	Assistance	Some Assistance	No Assistance	Assistance	Some Assistance	No Assistance	Assistance	Some Assistance	No Assistance	
pet													
chameleon													
change													
color													
end													
tail													
large													
follow													
bedroom													
beautiful													

Story 6

numerous
animals
land
breathe
air
birds
mammals
amphibians
lungs
gills

Tips for the Reading Facilitator:

Using a sheet of paper, cover all lines/sentences below the line/sentence the learner will read. Once the learner has read the line/sentence (with assistance or independently), uncover the next line/sentence. This technique offers less distraction and more focused attention on the line/sentence to be read.

After the learner reads each line/sentence (with or without assistance), provide positive reinforcement that is meaningful to the learner.
Be creative, use objects or video clips to help exemplify the words being learned.

Use the *Word List Data Sheet* that follows this story to track a learner's progress.

Use the *Master Word List Data Sheet* in the Appendix to track word recognition mastery.

Note: Words appearing in previous stories are regarded as being familiar to the learner. However, some review may be necessary to maintain word recognition and understanding.

The story with word symbols begins on the next page.

Numerous animals that live on land

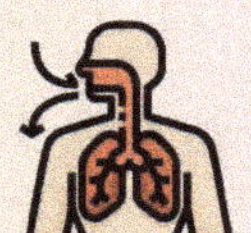  

or in water breathe air. Birds,

  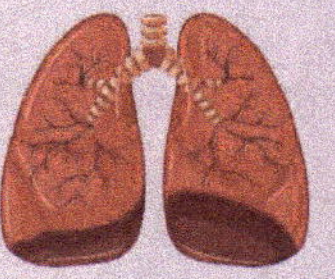

mammals, and amphibians have lungs

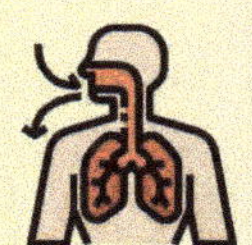 

to breathe air. Fish are also

animals but they use gills, not

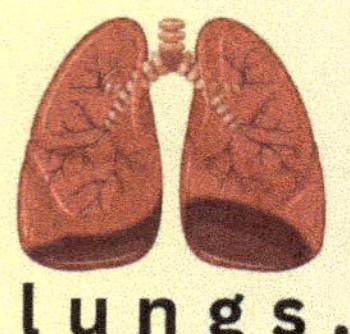

lungs.

Tips for the Reading Facilitator:

Once the learner can fluently read the story with word symbols, have them read the same story shown on the next page which eliminates individual word symbols.

Using a sheet of paper, cover all lines/sentences below the line/sentence the learner will read. Once the learner has read the line/sentence (with assistance or independently), uncover the next line/sentence. This technique offers less distraction and more focused attention on the line/sentence to be read.

After the learner reads each line/sentence (with or without assistance), provide positive reinforcement that is meaningful to the learner.

Be creative, use objects or video clips to help exemplify the words being learned.

Use the *Word List Data Sheet* that follows this story to track a learner's progress.

Use the *Master Word List Data Sheet* in the Appendix to track word recognition mastery.

Note: Words appearing in previous stories are regarded as being familiar to the learner. However, some review may be necessary to maintain word recognition and understanding.

Numerous animals that live on land or in water breathe air. Birds, mammals, and amphibians have lungs to breathe air. Fish are also animals but they use gills, not lungs.

Word List Data Sheets

(Copy this sheet as often as necessary to track progress over time)

Story 6 Words	Date:			Date:			Date:			Date:			The Date a Word is Mastered
	Assistance	Some Assistance	No Assistance	Assistance	Some Assistance	No Assistance	Assistance	Some Assistance	No Assistance	Assistance	Some Assistance	No Assistance	
numerous													
animals													
land													
breathe													
air													
birds													
mammals													
amphibians													
lungs													
gills													

Story 7

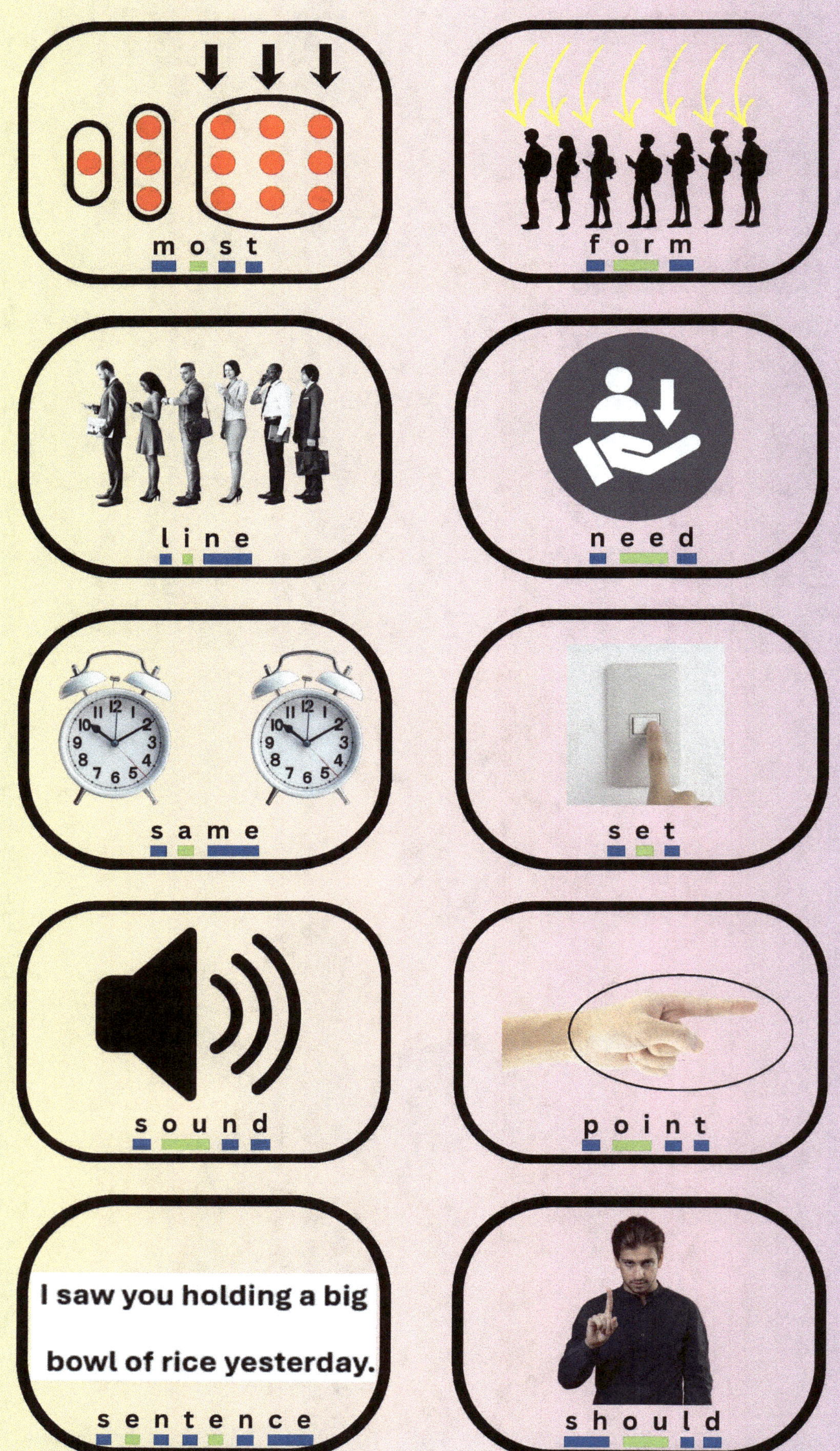
most
form
line
need
same
set
sound
point
I saw you holding a big
bowl of rice yesterday.
sentence
should

Tips for the Reading Facilitator:

Using a sheet of paper, cover all lines/sentences below the line/sentence the learner will read. Once the learner has read the line/sentence (with assistance or independently), uncover the next line/sentence. This technique offers less distraction and more focused attention on the line/sentence to be read.

After the learner reads each line/sentence (with or without assistance), provide positive reinforcement that is meaningful to the learner.
Be creative, use objects or video clips to help exemplify the words being learned.

Use the *Word List Data Sheet* that follows this story to track a learner's progress.

Use the *Master Word List Data Sheet* in the Appendix to track word recognition mastery.

Note: Words appearing in previous stories are regarded as being familiar to the learner. However, some review may be necessary to maintain word recognition and understanding.

The story with word symbols begins on the next page.

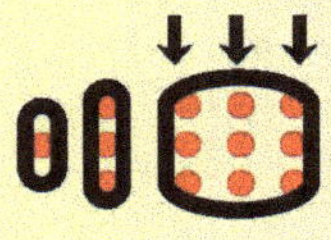  

Most people form a line when they

need to go into a store all at the

same time. The store workers set the

door bell sound to "on". Then, one of

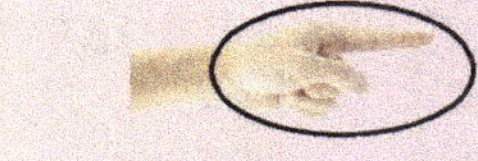

the store workers will point to the

people in line at the door and say

I saw you holding a big bowl of rice yesterday.

this sentence: "Come on in and it should

be a great day for all!"

Tips for the Reading Facilitator:

Once the learner can fluently read the story with word symbols, have them read the same story shown on the next page which eliminates individual word symbols.

Using a sheet of paper, cover all lines/sentences below the line/sentence the learner will read. Once the learner has read the line/sentence (with assistance or independently), uncover the next line/sentence. This technique offers less distraction and more focused attention on the line/sentence to be read.

After the learner reads each line/sentence (with or without assistance), provide positive reinforcement that is meaningful to the learner.

Be creative, use objects or video clips to help exemplify the words being learned.

Use the *Word List Data Sheet* that follows this story to track a learner's progress.

Use the *Master Word List Data Sheet* in the Appendix to track word recognition mastery.

Note: Words appearing in previous stories are regarded as being familiar to the learner. However, some review may be necessary to maintain word recognition and understanding.

Most people form a line when they need to go into a store all at the same time. The store workers set the door bell sound to “on”. Then, one of the store workers will point to the people in line at the door and say this sentence: “Come on in and it should be a great day for all!”

Word List Data Sheets

(Copy this sheet as often as necessary to track progress over time)

Story 7 Words	Date:			Date:			Date:			Date:			The Date a Word is Mastered
	Assistance	Some Assistance	No Assistance	Assistance	Some Assistance	No Assistance	Assistance	Some Assistance	No Assistance	Assistance	Some Assistance	No Assistance	
most													
form													
line													
need													
same													
set													
sound													
point													
sentence													
should													

Story 8

LPAEP
APPLE
learn
spell
through
2012
years
study
things
world
such
living
above

Tips for the Reading Facilitator:

Using a sheet of paper, cover all lines/sentences below the line/sentence the learner will read. Once the learner has read the line/sentence (with assistance or independently), uncover the next line/sentence. This technique offers less distraction and more focused attention on the line/sentence to be read.

After the learner reads each line/sentence (with or without assistance), provide positive reinforcement that is meaningful to the learner.
Be creative, use objects or video clips to help exemplify the words being learned.

Use the *Word List Data Sheet* that follows this story to track a learner's progress.

Use the *Master Word List Data Sheet* in the Appendix to track word recognition mastery.

Note: Words appearing in previous stories are regarded as being familiar to the learner. However, some review may be necessary to maintain word recognition and understanding.

The story with word symbols begins on the next page.

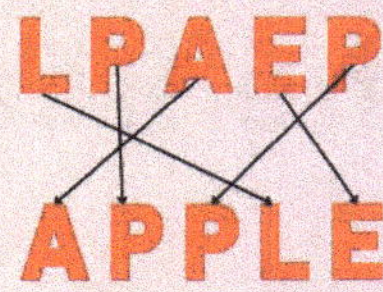

Children learn to spell many

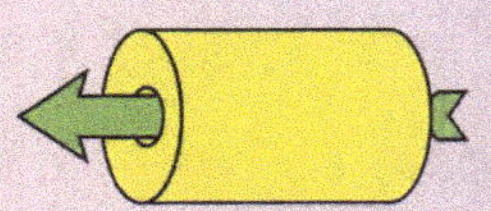

words over many years. Through

the years they study many things

about our world such as, "What

are living things?"

Above all, they learn how we

must look after the living things

on this world.

Tips for the Reading Facilitator:

Once the learner can fluently read the story with word symbols, have them read the same story shown on the next page which eliminates individual word symbols.

Using a sheet of paper, cover all lines/sentences below the line/sentence the learner will read. Once the learner has read the line/sentence (with assistance or independently), uncover the next line/sentence. This technique offers less distraction and more focused attention on the line/sentence to be read.

After the learner reads each line/sentence (with or without assistance), provide positive reinforcement that is meaningful to the learner.

Be creative, use objects or video clips to help exemplify the words being learned.

Use the *Word List Data Sheet* that follows this story to track a learner's progress.

Use the *Master Word List Data Sheet* in the Appendix to track word recognition mastery.

Note: Words appearing in previous stories are regarded as being familiar to the learner. However, some review may be necessary to maintain word recognition and understanding.

Children learn to spell many words over many years. Through the years they study many things about our world such as, “What are living things?”

Above all, they learn how we must look after the living things on this world.

Word List Data Sheets

(Copy this sheet as often as necessary to track progress over time)

Story 8 Words	Date:			Date:			Date:			Date:			The Date a Word is Mastered
	Assistance	Some Assistance	No Assistance	Assistance	Some Assistance	No Assistance	Assistance	Some Assistance	No Assistance	Assistance	Some Assistance	No Assistance	
learn													
spell													
years													
through													
study													
things													
world													
such													
living													
above													

Story 9

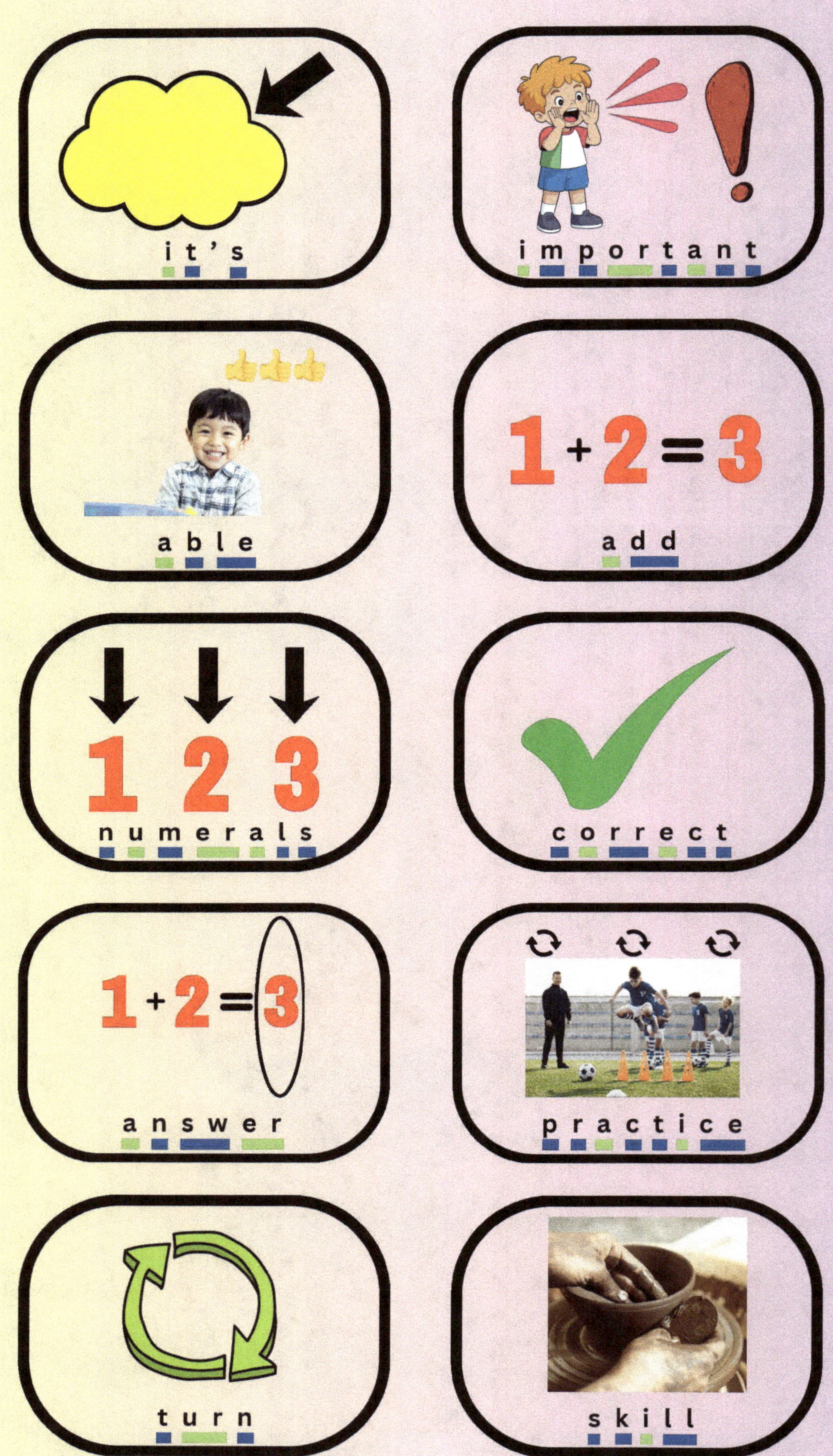

it's
important
able
1+2=3
add
1 2 3
numerals
correct
1+2=3
answer
practice
turn
skill

Tips for the Reading Facilitator:

Using a sheet of paper, cover all lines/sentences below the line/sentence the learner will read. Once the learner has read the line/sentence (with assistance or independently), uncover the next line/sentence. This technique offers less distraction and more focused attention on the line/sentence to be read.

After the learner reads each line/sentence (with or without assistance), provide positive reinforcement that is meaningful to the learner.
Be creative, use objects or video clips to help exemplify the words being learned.

Use the *Word List Data Sheet* that follows this story to track a learner's progress.

Use the *Master Word List Data Sheet* in the Appendix to track word recognition mastery.

Note: Words appearing in previous stories are regarded as being familiar to the learner. However, some review may be necessary to maintain word recognition and understanding.

The story with word symbols begins on the next page.

It's important to be able to

1+2=3 1 2 3

add numerals and get the

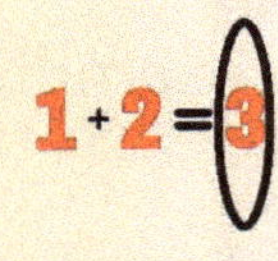

correct answer.

With practice you will turn this

into an important skill.

Tips for the Reading Facilitator:

Once the learner can fluently read the story with word symbols, have them read the same story shown on the next page which eliminates individual word symbols.

Using a sheet of paper, cover all lines/sentences below the line/sentence the learner will read. Once the learner has read the line/sentence (with assistance or independently), uncover the next line/sentence. This technique offers less distraction and more focused attention on the line/sentence to be read.

After the learner reads each line/sentence (with or without assistance), provide positive reinforcement that is meaningful to the learner.

Be creative, use objects or video clips to help exemplify the words being learned.

Use the *Word List Data Sheet* that follows this story to track a learner's progress.

Use the *Master Word List Data Sheet* in the Appendix to track word recognition mastery.

Note: Words appearing in previous stories are regarded as being familiar to the learner. However, some review may be necessary to maintain word recognition and understanding.

It’s important to be able to add numerals and get the correct answer.

With practice you will turn this into an important skill.

Word List Data Sheets

(Copy this sheet as often as necessary to track progress over time)

Story 9 Words	Date:			Date:			Date:			Date:			The Date a Word is Mastered
	Assistance	Some Assistance	No Assistance	Assistance	Some Assistance	No Assistance	Assistance	Some Assistance	No Assistance	Assistance	Some Assistance	No Assistance	
it's													
important													
able													
add													
numerals													
correct													
answer													
practice													
turn													
skill													

Story 10

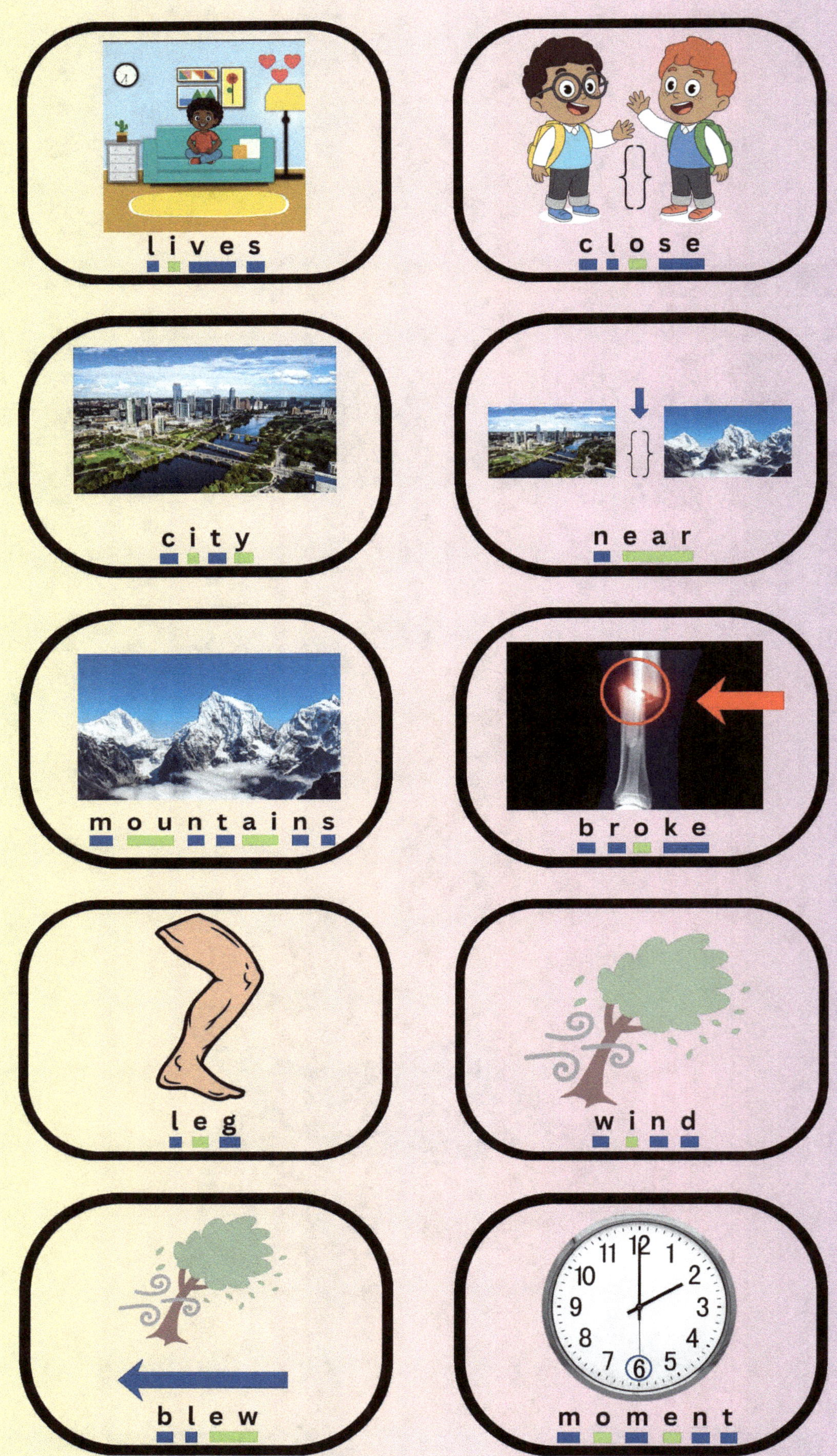
lives
close
city
near
mountains
broke
leg
wind
blew
moment

Tips for the Reading Facilitator:

Using a sheet of paper, cover all lines/sentences below the line/sentence the learner will read. Once the learner has read the line/sentence (with assistance or independently), uncover the next line/sentence. This technique offers less distraction and more focused attention on the line/sentence to be read.

After the learner reads each line/sentence (with or without assistance), provide positive reinforcement that is meaningful to the learner.
Be creative, use objects or video clips to help exemplify the words being learned.

Use the *Word List Data Sheet* that follows this story to track a learner's progress.

Use the *Master Word List Data Sheet* in the Appendix to track word recognition mastery.

Note: Words appearing in previous stories are regarded as being familiar to the learner. However, some review may be necessary to maintain word recognition and understanding.

The story with word symbols begins on the next page.

My friend lives close to a city

near the mountains.

Once, he broke his leg when

the wind blew him down.

He told me it was a very sore

moment for him.

Tips for the Reading Facilitator:

Once the learner can fluently read the story with word symbols, have them read the same story shown on the next page which eliminates individual word symbols.

Using a sheet of paper, cover all lines/sentences below the line/sentence the learner will read. Once the learner has read the line/sentence (with assistance or independently), uncover the next line/sentence. This technique offers less distraction and more focused attention on the line/sentence to be read.

After the learner reads each line/sentence (with or without assistance), provide positive reinforcement that is meaningful to the learner.

Be creative, use objects or video clips to help exemplify the words being learned.

Use the *Word List Data Sheet* that follows this story to track a learner's progress.

Use the *Master Word List Data Sheet* in the Appendix to track word recognition mastery.

Note: Words appearing in previous stories are regarded as being familiar to the learner. However, some review may be necessary to maintain word recognition and understanding.

My friend lives close to a city near mountains.

Once, he broke his leg when the wind blew him down.

He told me it was a very sore moment for him.

Word List Data Sheets

(Copy this sheet as often as necessary to track progress over time)

Story 10 Words	Date:			Date:			Date:			Date:			The Date a Word is Mastered
	Assistance	Some Assistance	No Assistance	Assistance	Some Assistance	No Assistance	Assistance	Some Assistance	No Assistance	Assistance	Some Assistance	No Assistance	
lives													
close													
city													
near													
mountains													
broke													
leg													
wind													
blew													
moment													

Story 11

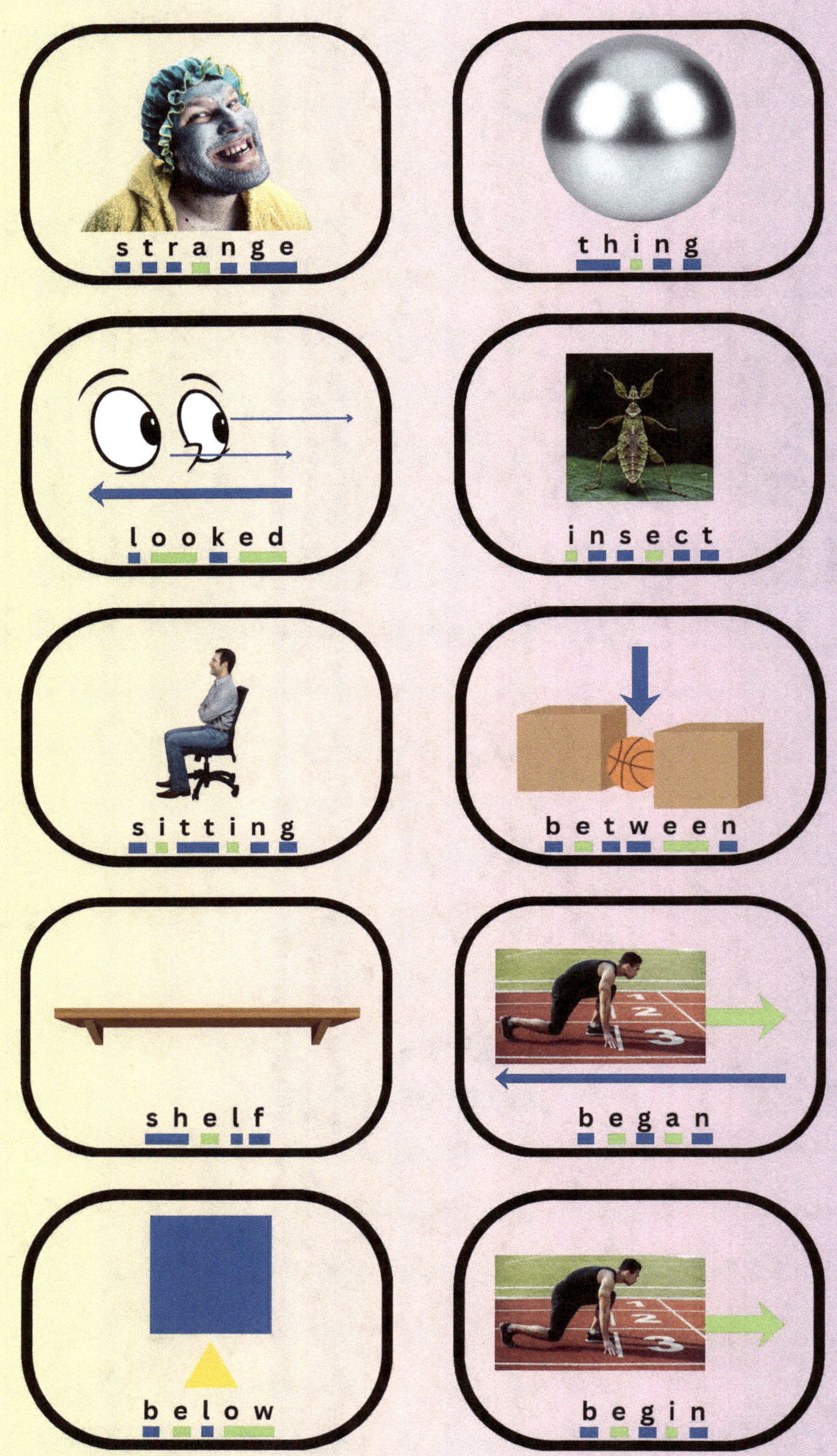
strange
thing
looked
insect
sitting
between
shelf
began
below
begin

Tips for the Reading Facilitator:

Using a sheet of paper, cover all lines/sentences below the line/sentence the learner will read. Once the learner has read the line/sentence (with assistance or independently), uncover the next line/sentence. This technique offers less distraction and more focused attention on the line/sentence to be read.

After the learner reads each line/sentence (with or without assistance), provide positive reinforcement that is meaningful to the learner.
Be creative, use objects or video clips to help exemplify the words being learned.

Use the *Word List Data Sheet* that follows this story to track a learner's progress.

Use the *Master Word List Data Sheet* in the Appendix to track word recognition mastery.

Note: Words appearing in previous stories are regarded as being familiar to the learner. However, some review may be necessary to maintain word recognition and understanding.

The story with word symbols begins on the next page.

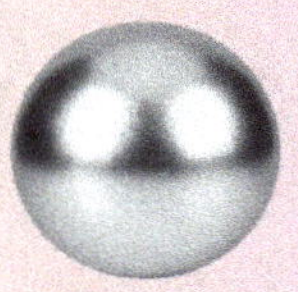
I saw a strange thing that

looked like an insect. It was

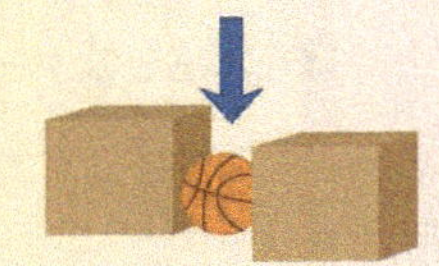
sitting between a book and a

doll on my friend's shelf. Then,

the thing began to walk. It

walked below the shelf onto a

green table. But I wanted the thing

to begin to walk out the door.

Tips for the Reading Facilitator:

Once the learner can fluently read the story with word symbols, have them read the same story shown on the next page which eliminates individual word symbols.

Using a sheet of paper, cover all lines/sentences below the line/sentence the learner will read. Once the learner has read the line/sentence (with assistance or independently), uncover the next line/sentence. This technique offers less distraction and more focused attention on the line/sentence to be read.

After the learner reads each line/sentence (with or without assistance), provide positive reinforcement that is meaningful to the learner.

Be creative, use objects or video clips to help exemplify the words being learned.

Use the *Word List Data Sheet* that follows this story to track a learner's progress.

Use the *Master Word List Data Sheet* in the Appendix to track word recognition mastery.

Note: Words appearing in previous stories are regarded as being familiar to the learner. However, some review may be necessary to maintain word recognition and understanding.

I saw a strange thing that looked like an insect. It was sitting between a book and a doll on my friend's shelf. Then, the thing began to walk. It walked below the shelf onto a green table. But I wanted the thing to begin to walk out the door.

Word List Data Sheets

(Copy this sheet as often as necessary to track progress over time)

Story 11 Words	Date:			Date:			Date:			Date:			The Date a Word is Mastered
	Assistance	Some Assistance	No Assistance	Assistance	Some Assistance	No Assistance	Assistance	Some Assistance	No Assistance	Assistance	Some Assistance	No Assistance	
strange													
thing													
looked													
insect													
sitting													
between													
shelf													
began													
below													
begin													

Story 12

country
earth
example
group
list
qualities
2
1
3
second
however
few
enough

Tips for the Reading Facilitator:

Using a sheet of paper, cover all lines/sentences below the line/sentence the learner will read. Once the learner has read the line/sentence (with assistance or independently), uncover the next line/sentence. This technique offers less distraction and more focused attention on the line/sentence to be read.

After the learner reads each line/sentence (with or without assistance), provide positive reinforcement that is meaningful to the learner.
Be creative, use objects or video clips to help exemplify the words being learned.

Use the *Word List Data Sheet* that follows this story to track a learner's progress.

Use the *Master Word List Data Sheet* in the Appendix to track word recognition mastery.

Note: Words appearing in previous stories are regarded as being familiar to the learner. However, some review may be necessary to maintain word recognition and understanding.

The story with word symbols begins on the next page.

Some people think the country they live in

is the best country on earth. For example,

one group of people can list all the good

qualities they can think of about their

country. But, a second group of people can

also list just as many good qualities about

  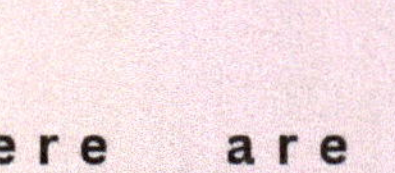 

their country. However, there are a few people

who cannot think of enough qualities they love

about their country to make as long a list as other people.

Tips for the Reading Facilitator:

Once the learner can fluently read the story with word symbols, have them read the same story shown on the next page which eliminates individual word symbols.

Using a sheet of paper, cover all lines/sentences below the line/sentence the learner will read. Once the learner has read the line/sentence (with assistance or independently), uncover the next line/sentence. This technique offers less distraction and more focused attention on the line/sentence to be read.

After the learner reads each line/sentence (with or without assistance), provide positive reinforcement that is meaningful to the learner.

Be creative, use objects or video clips to help exemplify the words being learned.

Use the *Word List Data Sheet* that follows this story to track a learner's progress.

Use the *Master Word List Data Sheet* in the Appendix to track word recognition mastery.

Note: Words appearing in previous stories are regarded as being familiar to the learner. However, some review may be necessary to maintain word recognition and understanding.

Some people think the country they live in is the best country on earth. For example, one group of people can list all the good qualities they can think of about their country. But, a second group of people can list just as many good qualities about their country. However, there are a few people who cannot think of enough qualities they love about their country to make as long a list as other people.

Word List Data Sheets

(Copy this sheet as often as necessary to track progress over time)

Story 12 Words	Date:			Date:			Date:			Date:			The Date a Word is Mastered
	Assistance	Some Assistance	No Assistance	Assistance	Some Assistance	No Assistance	Assistance	Some Assistance	No Assistance	Assistance	Some Assistance	No Assistance	
country													
earth													
example													
group													
list													
qualities													
second													
however													
few													
enough													

Story 13

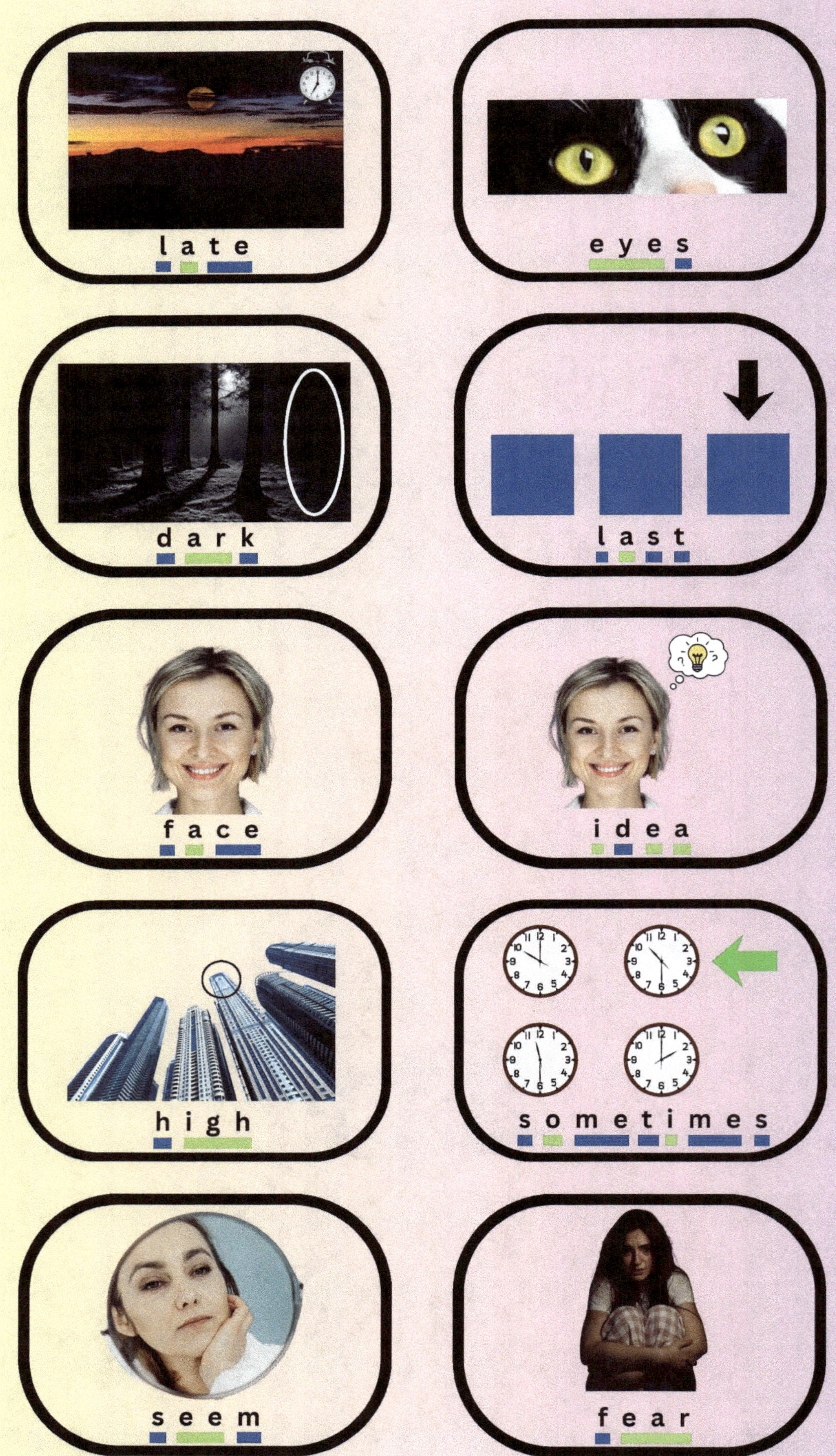
late
eyes
dark
last
face
idea
high
sometimes
seem
fear

Tips for the Reading Facilitator:

Using a sheet of paper, cover all lines/sentences below the line/sentence the learner will read. Once the learner has read the line/sentence (with assistance or independently), uncover the next line/sentence. This technique offers less distraction and more focused attention on the line/sentence to be read.

After the learner reads each line/sentence (with or without assistance), provide positive reinforcement that is meaningful to the learner.
Be creative, use objects or video clips to help exemplify the words being learned.

Use the *Word List Data Sheet* that follows this story to track a learner's progress.

Use the *Master Word List Data Sheet* in the Appendix to track word recognition mastery.

Note: Words appearing in previous stories are regarded as being familiar to the learner. However, some review may be necessary to maintain word recognition and understanding.

The story with word symbols begins on the next page.

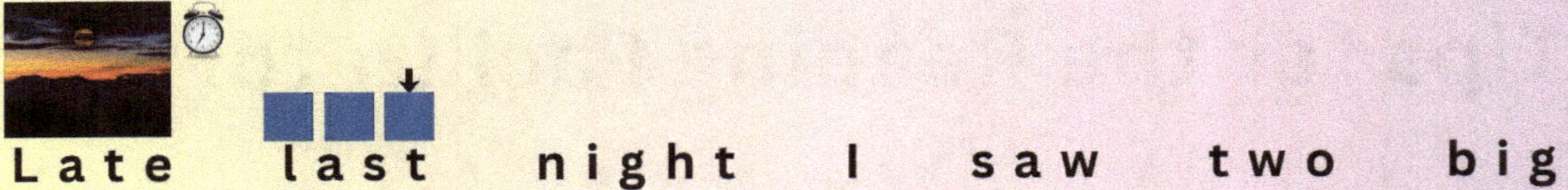

Late last night I saw two big

round yellow eyes in the dark.

I could not see a face, just

the yellow eyes. I had the idea

of running away. But then the

yellow eyes looked like they

jumped high up on a fence.

Sometimes I seem to fear what I

cannot see.

Tips for the Reading Facilitator:

Once the learner can fluently read the story with word symbols, have them read the same story shown on the next page which eliminates individual word symbols.

Using a sheet of paper, cover all lines/sentences below the line/sentence the learner will read. Once the learner has read the line/sentence (with assistance or independently), uncover the next line/sentence. This technique offers less distraction and more focused attention on the line/sentence to be read.

After the learner reads each line/sentence (with or without assistance), provide positive reinforcement that is meaningful to the learner.

Be creative, use objects or video clips to help exemplify the words being learned.

Use the *Word List Data Sheet* that follows this story to track a learner's progress.

Use the *Master Word List Data Sheet* in the Appendix to track word recognition mastery.

Note: Words appearing in previous stories are regarded as being familiar to the learner. However, some review may be necessary to maintain word recognition and understanding.

Late last night I saw two big round yellow eyes in the dark. I could not see a face, just the yellow eyes. I had the idea of running away. But then the yellow eyes looked like they jumped high up on a fence. Sometimes I seem to fear what I cannot see.

Word List Data Sheets

(Copy this sheet as often as necessary to track progress over time)

Story 13 Words	Date:			Date:			Date:			Date:			The Date a Word is Mastered
	Assistance	Some Assistance	No Assistance	Assistance	Some Assistance	No Assistance	Assistance	Some Assistance	No Assistance	Assistance	Some Assistance	No Assistance	
late													
eyes													
dark													
last													
face													
idea													
high													
sometimes													
seem													
fear													

Story 14

leave
Sun Mon Tue Wed Thu Fri Sat
often
really
hope
might
plant
young
took
miss
planting

Tips for the Reading Facilitator:

Using a sheet of paper, cover all lines/sentences below the line/sentence the learner will read. Once the learner has read the line/sentence (with assistance or independently), uncover the next line/sentence. This technique offers less distraction and more focused attention on the line/sentence to be read.

After the learner reads each line/sentence (with or without assistance), provide positive reinforcement that is meaningful to the learner.
Be creative, use objects or video clips to help exemplify the words being learned.

Use the *Word List Data Sheet* that follows this story to track a learner's progress.

Use the *Master Word List Data Sheet* in the Appendix to track word recognition mastery.

Note: Words appearing in previous stories are regarded as being familiar to the learner. However, some review may be necessary to maintain word recognition and understanding.

The story with word symbols begins on the next page.

Before I leave home for the day, I

often make a list of the things I

really hope to get done. Today, I might

plant a young tree because I took one

home from my tree farm yesterday. "Plant

the tree", is on my list for today. I

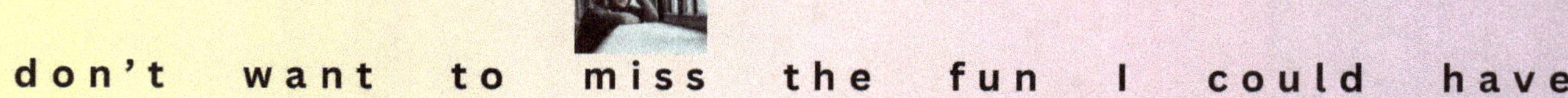

don't want to miss the fun I could have

planting my young tree.

Tips for the Reading Facilitator:

Once the learner can fluently read the story with word symbols, have them read the same story shown on the next page which eliminates individual word symbols.

Using a sheet of paper, cover all lines/sentences below the line/sentence the learner will read. Once the learner has read the line/sentence (with assistance or independently), uncover the next line/sentence. This technique offers less distraction and more focused attention on the line/sentence to be read.

After the learner reads each line/sentence (with or without assistance), provide positive reinforcement that is meaningful to the learner.

Be creative, use objects or video clips to help exemplify the words being learned.

Use the *Word List Data Sheet* that follows this story to track a learner's progress.

Use the *Master Word List Data Sheet* in the Appendix to track word recognition mastery.

Note: Words appearing in previous stories are regarded as being familiar to the learner. However, some review may be necessary to maintain word recognition and understanding.

Before I leave home for the day I often make a list of the things I really hope to get done. Today, I might plant a young tree because I took one home from my tree farm yesterday. "Plant the tree", is on my list for today. I don't want to miss the fun I could have planting my young tree.

Word List Data Sheets

(Copy this sheet as often as necessary to track progress over time)

Story 14 Words	Date:			Date:			Date:			Date:			The Date a Word is Mastered
	Assistance	Some Assistance	No Assistance	Assistance	Some Assistance	No Assistance	Assistance	Some Assistance	No Assistance	Assistance	Some Assistance	No Assistance	
leave													
often													
really													
hope													
might													
plant													
young													
took													
miss													
planting													

Story 15

talk
life
thought
something
share
story
42
mile
side
without
become

Tips for the Reading Facilitator:

Using a sheet of paper, cover all lines/sentences below the line/sentence the learner will read. Once the learner has read the line/sentence (with assistance or independently), uncover the next line/sentence. This technique offers less distraction and more focused attention on the line/sentence to be read.

After the learner reads each line/sentence (with or without assistance), provide positive reinforcement that is meaningful to the learner.
Be creative, use objects or video clips to help exemplify the words being learned.

Use the *Word List Data Sheet* that follows this story to track a learner's progress.

Use the *Master Word List Data Sheet* in the Appendix to track word recognition mastery.

Note: Words appearing in previous stories are regarded as being familiar to the learner. However, some review may be necessary to maintain word recognition and understanding.

The story with word symbols begins on the next page.

My friend and I talk together about life often. One of us will have a thought about something to do with life. Then, we each share our thought in a story.

But, we can also walk a mile side by side without any words to say.

I feel happy when I hear my friend share his thought, "Life has become better with a good friend like you by my side."

Tips for the Reading Facilitator:

Once the learner can fluently read the story with word symbols, have them read the same story shown on the next page which eliminates individual word symbols.

Using a sheet of paper, cover all lines/sentences below the line/sentence the learner will read. Once the learner has read the line/sentence (with assistance or independently), uncover the next line/sentence. This technique offers less distraction and more focused attention on the line/sentence to be read.

After the learner reads each line/sentence (with or without assistance), provide positive reinforcement that is meaningful to the learner.

Be creative, use objects or video clips to help exemplify the words being learned.

Use the *Word List Data Sheet* that follows this story to track a learner's progress.

Use the *Master Word List Data Sheet* in the Appendix to track word recognition mastery.

Note: Words appearing in previous stories are regarded as being familiar to the learner. However, some review may be necessary to maintain word recognition and understanding.

My friend and I talk together about life often. One of us will have a thought about something to do with life. Then, we each share our thought in a story. But, we can also walk a mile side by side without any words to say. I feel happy when I hear my friend share his thought, “Life has become better with a good friend like you by my side.”

Word List Data Sheets

(Copy this sheet as often as necessary to track progress over time)

Story 15 Words	Date:			Date:			Date:			Date:			The Date a Word is Mastered
	Assistance	Some Assistance	No Assistance	Assistance	Some Assistance	No Assistance	Assistance	Some Assistance	No Assistance	Assistance	Some Assistance	No Assistance	
talk													
life													
thought													
something													
share													
story													
mile													
side													
without													
become													

Story 16

during
early
12
1
2
3
4
5
6
7
8
9
10
11
hours
24h
cried
body
covered
blanket
didn't
certain
complete

Tips for the Reading Facilitator:

Using a sheet of paper, cover all lines/sentences below the line/sentence the learner will read. Once the learner has read the line/sentence (with assistance or independently), uncover the next line/sentence. This technique offers less distraction and more focused attention on the line/sentence to be read.

After the learner reads each line/sentence (with or without assistance), provide positive reinforcement that is meaningful to the learner.
Be creative, use objects or video clips to help exemplify the words being learned.

Use the *Word List Data Sheet* that follows this story to track a learner's progress.

Use the *Master Word List Data Sheet* in the Appendix to track word recognition mastery.

Note: Words appearing in previous stories are regarded as being familiar to the learner. However, some review may be necessary to maintain word recognition and understanding.

The story with word symbols begins on the next page.

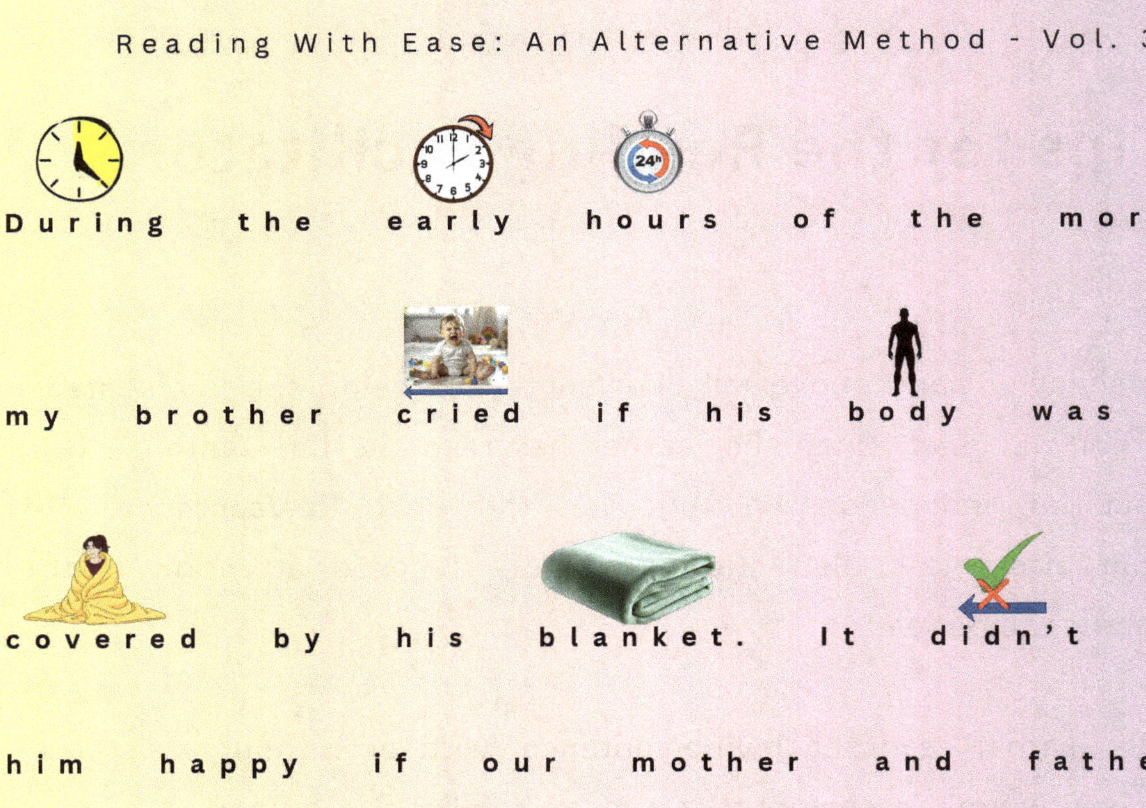

During the early hours of the morning, my brother cried if his body was not covered by his blanket. It didn't make him happy if our mother and father

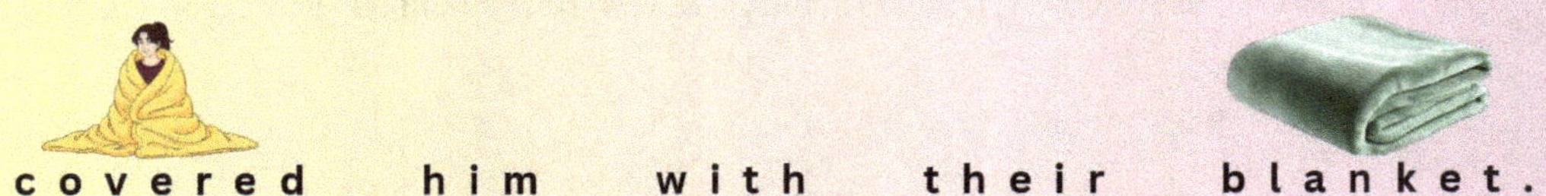

covered him with their blanket.

Only a certain blanket would do. My brother would only feel complete and

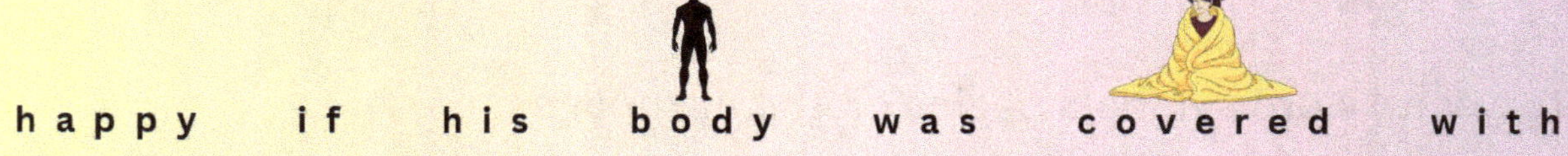

happy if his body was covered with

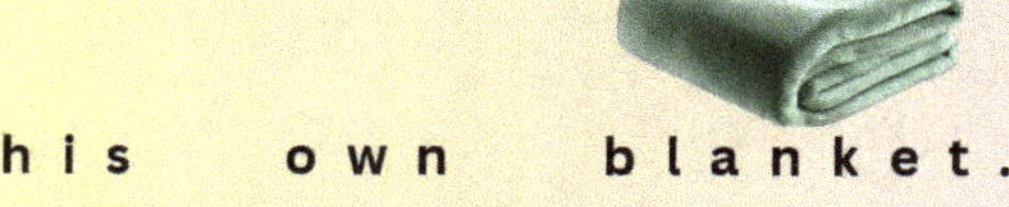

his own blanket.

Tips for the Reading Facilitator:

Once the learner can fluently read the story with word symbols, have them read the same story shown on the next page which eliminates individual word symbols.

Using a sheet of paper, cover all lines/sentences below the line/sentence the learner will read. Once the learner has read the line/sentence (with assistance or independently), uncover the next line/sentence. This technique offers less distraction and more focused attention on the line/sentence to be read.

After the learner reads each line/sentence (with or without assistance), provide positive reinforcement that is meaningful to the learner.

Be creative, use objects or video clips to help exemplify the words being learned.

Use the *Word List Data Sheet* that follows this story to track a learner's progress.

Use the *Master Word List Data Sheet* in the Appendix to track word recognition mastery.

Note: Words appearing in previous stories are regarded as being familiar to the learner. However, some review may be necessary to maintain word recognition and understanding.

During the early hours of the morning, my brother cried if his body was not covered by his blanket. It didn't make him happy if our mother and father covered him with their blanket. Only a certain blanket would do. My brother would only feel complete and happy if his body was covered with his own blanket.

Word List Data Sheets

(Copy this sheet as often as necessary to track progress over time)

Story 16 Words	Date:			Date:			Date:			Date:			The Date a Word is Mastered
	Assistance	Some Assistance	No Assistance	Assistance	Some Assistance	No Assistance	Assistance	Some Assistance	No Assistance	Assistance	Some Assistance	No Assistance	
during													
early													
hours													
cried													
body													
covered													
blanket													
didn't													
certain													
complete													

Story 17

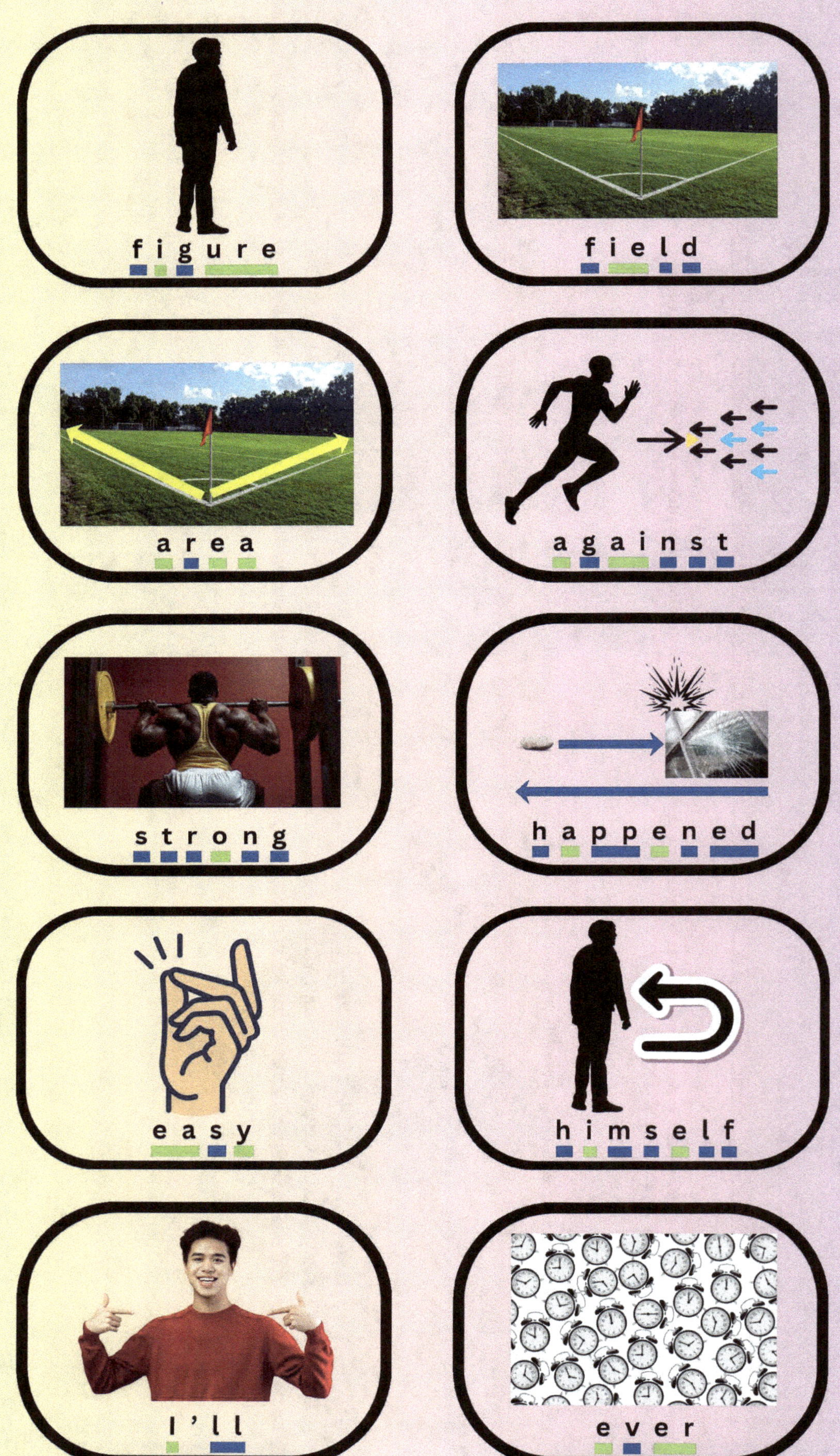
figure
field
area
against
strong
happened
easy
himself
I'll
ever

Tips for the Reading Facilitator:

Using a sheet of paper, cover all lines/sentences below the line/sentence the learner will read. Once the learner has read the line/sentence (with assistance or independently), uncover the next line/sentence. This technique offers less distraction and more focused attention on the line/sentence to be read.

After the learner reads each line/sentence (with or without assistance), provide positive reinforcement that is meaningful to the learner.
Be creative, use objects or video clips to help exemplify the words being learned.

Use the *Word List Data Sheet* that follows this story to track a learner's progress.

Use the *Master Word List Data Sheet* in the Appendix to track word recognition mastery.

Note: Words appearing in previous stories are regarded as being familiar to the learner. However, some review may be necessary to maintain word recognition and understanding.

The story with word symbols begins on the next page.

One day, my friend and I saw a far off figure run across the school field. The field area is immense! The figure ran against a strong wind. But the figure happened to make it look like an easy run. Tomorrow, my friend will try to run across the field by himself. I don't think I'll ever try running across that field. Running is not my favorite thing to do.

Tips for the Reading Facilitator:

Once the learner can fluently read the story with word symbols, have them read the same story shown on the next page which eliminates individual word symbols.

Using a sheet of paper, cover all lines/sentences below the line/sentence the learner will read. Once the learner has read the line/sentence (with assistance or independently), uncover the next line/sentence. This technique offers less distraction and more focused attention on the line/sentence to be read.

After the learner reads each line/sentence (with or without assistance), provide positive reinforcement that is meaningful to the learner.

Be creative, use objects or video clips to help exemplify the words being learned.

Use the *Word List Data Sheet* that follows this story to track a learner's progress.

Use the *Master Word List Data Sheet* in the Appendix to track word recognition mastery.

Note: Words appearing in previous stories are regarded as being familiar to the learner. However, some review may be necessary to maintain word recognition and understanding.

One day, my friend and I saw a far off figure run across the school field. The field area is immense! The figure ran against a strong wind. But the figure happened to make it look like an easy run. Tomorrow, my friend will try to run across the field by himself. I don't think I'll ever try running across that field. Running is not my favorite thing to do.

Word List Data Sheets

(Copy this sheet as often as necessary to track progress over time)

Story 17 Words	Date:			Date:			Date:			Date:			The Date a Word is Mastered
	Assistance	Some Assistance	No Assistance	Assistance	Some Assistance	No Assistance	Assistance	Some Assistance	No Assistance	Assistance	Some Assistance	No Assistance	
figure													
field													
area													
against													
strong													
happened													
easy													
himself													
I'll													
ever													

Story 18

king
heard
She was cheating in the exam.
told
hundred
listen
plan
knew
order
passed
music

Tips for the Reading Facilitator:

Using a sheet of paper, cover all lines/sentences below the line/sentence the learner will read. Once the learner has read the line/sentence (with assistance or independently), uncover the next line/sentence. This technique offers less distraction and more focused attention on the line/sentence to be read.

After the learner reads each line/sentence (with or without assistance), provide positive reinforcement that is meaningful to the learner.
Be creative, use objects or video clips to help exemplify the words being learned.

Use the *Word List Data Sheet* that follows this story to track a learner's progress.

Use the *Master Word List Data Sheet* in the Appendix to track word recognition mastery.

Note: Words appearing in previous stories are regarded as being familiar to the learner. However, some review may be necessary to maintain word recognition and understanding.

The story with word symbols begins on the next page.

The king of a far off country heard many sad stories told by more than a hundred of his people. The king would listen to each story. Then, he made a plan to help all his people. The king knew his plan would make life better for his people. Once the order for the plan was passed, the people were heard to sing over many days. The king heard the music of his happy people. This made the king happy also.

Tips for the Reading Facilitator:

Once the learner can fluently read the story with word symbols, have them read the same story shown on the next page which eliminates individual word symbols.

Using a sheet of paper, cover all lines/sentences below the line/sentence the learner will read. Once the learner has read the line/sentence (with assistance or independently), uncover the next line/sentence. This technique offers less distraction and more focused attention on the line/sentence to be read.

After the learner reads each line/sentence (with or without assistance), provide positive reinforcement that is meaningful to the learner.

Be creative, use objects or video clips to help exemplify the words being learned.

Use the *Word List Data Sheet* that follows this story to track a learner's progress.

Use the *Master Word List Data Sheet* in the Appendix to track word recognition mastery.

Note: Words appearing in previous stories are regarded as being familiar to the learner. However, some review may be necessary to maintain word recognition and understanding.

The king of a far off country heard many sad stories told by more than a hundred of his people. The king would listen to each story. Then, he made a plan to help all his people. The king knew his plan would make life better for his people. Once the order for the plan was passed, the people were heard to sing over many days. The king heard the music of his happy people. This made the king happy also.

Word List Data Sheets

(Copy this sheet as often as necessary to track progress over time)

Story 18 Words	Date:			Date:			Date:			Date:			The Date a Word is Mastered
	Assistance	Some Assistance	No Assistance	Assistance	Some Assistance	No Assistance	Assistance	Some Assistance	No Assistance	Assistance	Some Assistance	No Assistance	
king													
heard													
told													
hundred													
listen													
plan													
knew													
order													
passed													
music													

Story 19

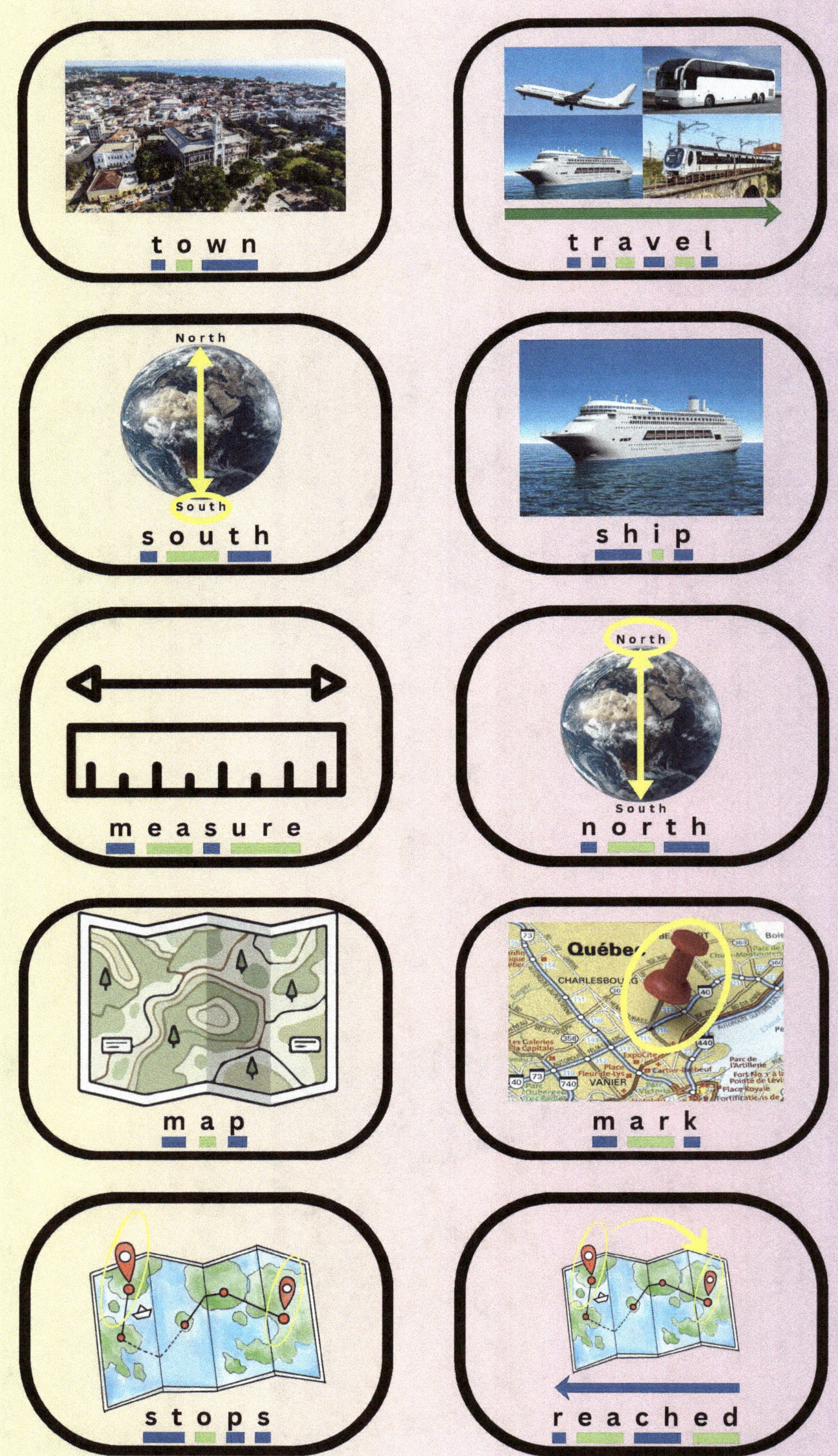
town
travel
North
South
south
ship
measure
North
South
north
Québec
CHARLESBOURG
VANIER
map
mark
stops
reached

Tips for the Reading Facilitator:

Using a sheet of paper, cover all lines/sentences below the line/sentence the learner will read. Once the learner has read the line/sentence (with assistance or independently), uncover the next line/sentence. This technique offers less distraction and more focused attention on the line/sentence to be read.

After the learner reads each line/sentence (with or without assistance), provide positive reinforcement that is meaningful to the learner.
Be creative, use objects or video clips to help exemplify the words being learned.

Use the *Word List Data Sheet* that follows this story to track a learner's progress.

Use the *Master Word List Data Sheet* in the Appendix to track word recognition mastery.

Note: Words appearing in previous stories are regarded as being familiar to the learner. However, some review may be necessary to maintain word recognition and understanding.

The story with word symbols begins on the next page.

Sometimes, some of the people I know from my

town travel south by ship to get away from

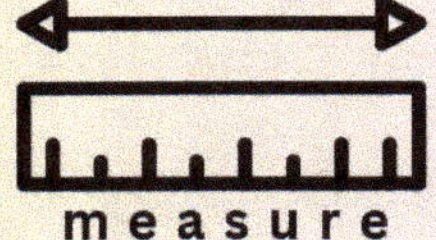 

the cold. They measure how far they travel from

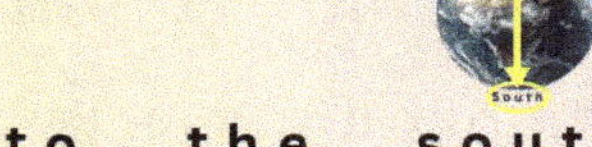 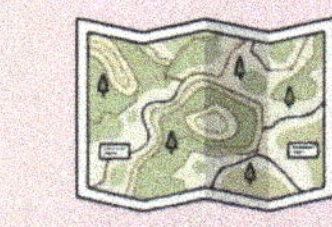

the north to the south on a map. Along the

way, they mark the stops the ship makes on

their map. When they have reached the town

in the south, they enjoy the warm sun.

Tips for the Reading Facilitator:

Once the learner can fluently read the story with word symbols, have them read the same story shown on the next page which eliminates individual word symbols.

Using a sheet of paper, cover all lines/sentences below the line/sentence the learner will read. Once the learner has read the line/sentence (with assistance or independently), uncover the next line/sentence. This technique offers less distraction and more focused attention on the line/sentence to be read.

After the learner reads each line/sentence (with or without assistance), provide positive reinforcement that is meaningful to the learner.

Be creative, use objects or video clips to help exemplify the words being learned.

Use the *Word List Data Sheet* that follows this story to track a learner's progress.

Use the *Master Word List Data Sheet* in the Appendix to track word recognition mastery.

Note: Words appearing in previous stories are regarded as being familiar to the learner. However, some review may be necessary to maintain word recognition and understanding.

Sometimes, some of the people I know from my town travel south by ship to get away from the cold. They measure how far they travel from the north to the south on a map. Along the way, they mark the stops the ship makes on their map. When they have reached the town in the south, they enjoy the warm sun.

Word List Data Sheets

(Copy this sheet as often as necessary to track progress over time)

Story 19 Words	Date:			Date:			Date:			Date:			The Date a Word is Mastered
	Assistance	Some Assistance	No Assistance	Assistance	Some Assistance	No Assistance	Assistance	Some Assistance	No Assistance	Assistance	Some Assistance	No Assistance	
town													
travel													
south													
ship													
measure													
north													
map													
mark													
stops													
reached													

Story 20

sure
notice
piece
pattern
low
remember
seen
several
products
even

Tips for the Reading Facilitator:

Using a sheet of paper, cover all lines/sentences below the line/sentence the learner will read. Once the learner has read the line/sentence (with assistance or independently), uncover the next line/sentence. This technique offers less distraction and more focused attention on the line/sentence to be read.

After the learner reads each line/sentence (with or without assistance), provide positive reinforcement that is meaningful to the learner.
Be creative, use objects or video clips to help exemplify the words being learned.

Use the *Word List Data Sheet* that follows this story to track a learner's progress.

Use the *Master Word List Data Sheet* in the Appendix to track word recognition mastery.

Note: Words appearing in previous stories are regarded as being familiar to the learner. However, some review may be necessary to maintain word recognition and understanding.

The story with word symbols begins on the next page.

 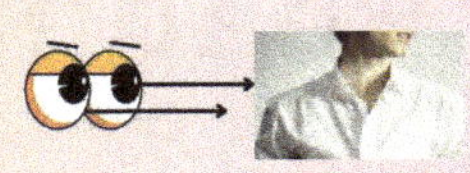

He is sure to notice that the

top piece of that pattern is too

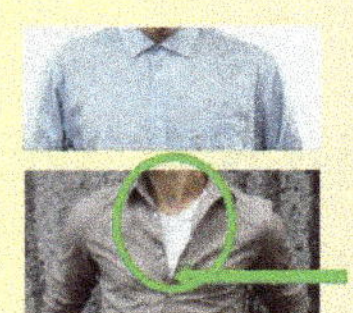 

low on the coat. Remember, he

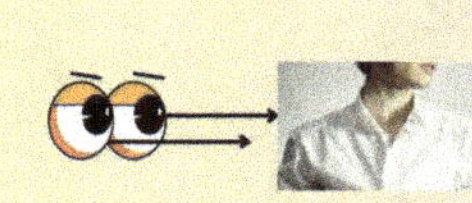 

has seen several good coat

products. And also, please remember

the pattern must be even for him

to like it.

Tips for the Reading Facilitator:

Once the learner can fluently read the story with word symbols, have them read the same story shown on the next page which eliminates individual word symbols.

Using a sheet of paper, cover all lines/sentences below the line/sentence the learner will read. Once the learner has read the line/sentence (with assistance or independently), uncover the next line/sentence. This technique offers less distraction and more focused attention on the line/sentence to be read.

After the learner reads each line/sentence (with or without assistance), provide positive reinforcement that is meaningful to the learner.

Be creative, use objects or video clips to help exemplify the words being learned.

Use the *Word List Data Sheet* that follows this story to track a learner's progress.

Use the *Master Word List Data Sheet* in the Appendix to track word recognition mastery.

Note: Words appearing in previous stories are regarded as being familiar to the learner. However, some review may be necessary to maintain word recognition and understanding.

He is sure to notice that the top piece of that pattern is too low on the coat. Remember, he has seen several good coat products. And also, please remember, the coat pattern must be even for him to like it.

Word List Data Sheets

(Copy this sheet as often as necessary to track progress over time)

Story 20 Words	Date:			Date:			Date:			Date:			The Date a Word is Mastered
	Assistance	Some Assistance	No Assistance	Assistance	Some Assistance	No Assistance	Assistance	Some Assistance	No Assistance	Assistance	Some Assistance	No Assistance	
sure													
notice													
piece													
pattern													
low													
remember													
seen													
several													
products													
even													

Spelling Made Fun!

Congratulations!

The first level of reading based on the most frequent words in print (according to Dolch and Fry) is done. However, achieving mastery comes with practice. So, reading practice is worthwhile. Something to help achieve mastery is learning to spell each of the two hundred words in this alternative reading guide. Starting with the short words is best. However, following the interest of the learner is also best practice.

Here is an example of the procedure to encouraging spelling:

1. The learner selects a word of interest.

2. The facilitator (or the learner) prints each letter of the word on separate post-it notes. (Modification: The learner can use sheets of sticker alphabet letters, placing each letter of a word on separate post-it notes.) See Figure 1 on the next page.

3. The facilitator scrambles the post-it notes.

4. With the pictured word in sight, the facilitator demonstrates to the learner the procedure of unscrambling the letter post-it notes to match the letter order in the word of choice, phonetically pronouncing each letter as it is placed in sequence.

5. The facilitator says to the learner. “Now it is your turn to place each letter in order matching the letter order of the word you chose.”

6. The facilitator may assist the learner's eye tracking using a pencil or other pointer type object to redirect as needed. Practice as many times as necessary to fade support until the learner is unscrambling the post-it note letters to spell the word independently.

7. The last step is to remove the picture word card completely from view and have the learner unscramble the post-it notes' letters with phonetical assistance as needed. Practice until the learner is unscrambling the letters independently.

Give positive reinforcement to encourage further spelling ventures. Figure 1 below provides an example of this alternative learning to spell procedure.

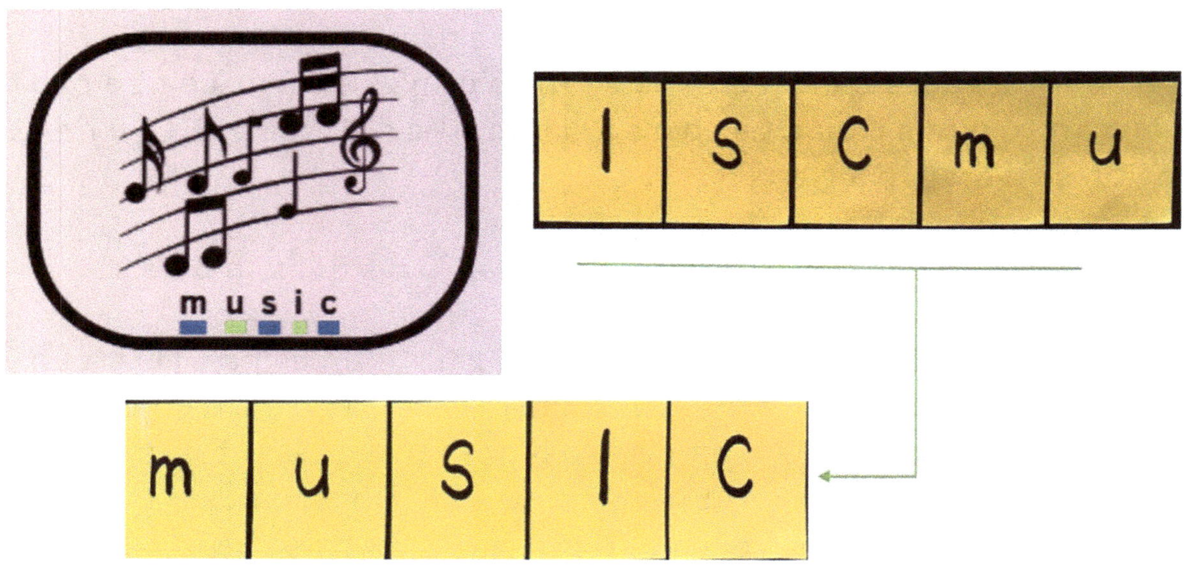

Delve Deeper into the Origins of Words

If an individual is interested in knowing more about the origins and/or definitions of any particular word, the facilitator can model how to search for the word using www.dictionary.com, a dictionary app, or a book style dictionary can be helpful. Encourage and support an individual's curiosity—it is the doorway to continuous, life-long learning.

Verb example:

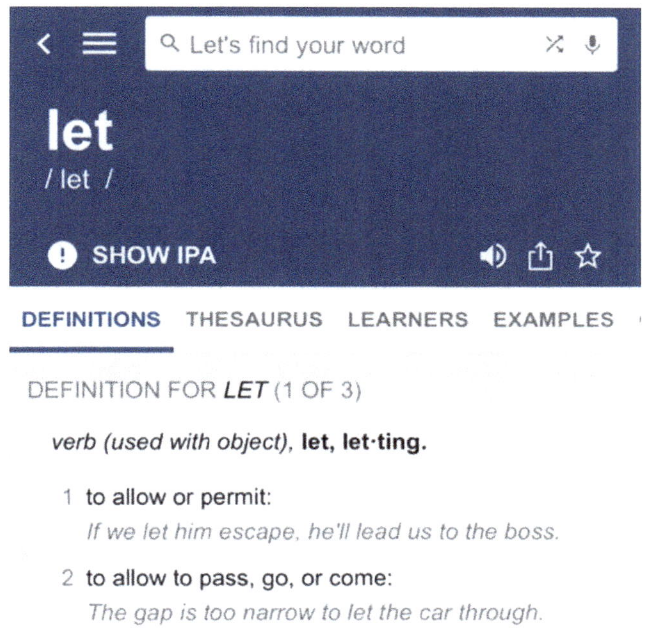

Sentence Building (Mirroring)

Here is a fun way for an individual to practice building sentences:

1. The individual chooses a story to use as the model for their sentence building.
2. The individual chooses a sentence from within the model story to mirror.
3. Gather all the Word Cards necessary for the individual to mirror the sentence from the model story chosen. Framing (i.e., the facilitator assists the individual to select the Word Cards needed from a smaller pre-selected group of Word Cards) the selection of Word Cards is the best place to start. The goal: Over time and practice, the individual will be able to select Word Cards from among several more on their own.
4. The individual builds a sentence that mirrors the sentence they chose from within the model story, with assistance as needed. Fade support and prompts gradually. NOTE: Fading support is the process of gradually reducing the quantity and type of support given to a learner to complete part of or all of a task or activity. The goal is for the learner to complete a task or activity independently. *An example of fading support is transitioning from hand-over-hand paired with verbal cues; to a light touch on the learner's elbow with verbal cues; to pointing with verbal cues; to verbal cues only; to pointing as needed only; to no prompts or cues at all.*

5. Practice this procedure for several more sentences until the individual demonstrates sentence mirroring mastery (i.e., no support or prompts are given by the facilitator).

Sentence Building (Freestyle)

Enabling successful freestyle sentence building using Word Cards available from one or more stories within this and previous facilitation guides requires backward planning. The facilitator, who has learned which words the learner knows well, begins by framing (pre-selecting) Word Cards that the individual would be able to use for building their own, unique sentence of six or more words. With practice, the individual will create their own sentence using more Word Cards, until pre-selecting/framing choices are no longer available.

A six-word sentence example: **They show kindness to all animals.**

A ten-word sentence example: **On my birthday I am hoping for a large blanket.**

Inferencing Skill Building

Assisting a learner to improve inferencing/critical thinking skills regarding the content of each story utilizes broad and versatile inquiries using: **Who…**, **What…**, **Where…**, **When…**, **Why…**, **How…**

Examples of inferencing/critical thinking skill building inquiries:

Story 1: Tell me **what** was in the story window? Tell me **who** wanted to ride a new red bike? Tell me **how** does it feel to ride a new bike?

Story 2: Tell me **why** you would wear a coat? Tell me **how** wearing a coat is good for us? Tell me **when** wearing a coat could be bad for us?

Story 3: Tell me **what** kind of food do the birds you've seen eat? Tell me **where** have you seen a bird's nest?

Story 4: Tell me **when** has someone let you buy something special that you wanted? Tell me **where** you were and **who** was it that let you buy something special that you wanted?

Story 5: Tell me **how** could a door appear to open by itself? Tell me **where** have you seen a door appear to open by itself?

Parts of Speech: Classifying Words as Nouns and Pronouns

Parts of Speech: Classifying Words as Nouns, Pronouns, and Verbs

Assisting a learner increase their skill of recognizing parts of speech is an important ability that improves reading comprehension and writing competency.

In this Reading with Ease: An Alternative Method, volume 3 classifying words into the first three of eight parts of speech provides a good foundation. Scaffold learner support [i.e., fading support over time] using the word picture cards from volumes 1, 2, and 3 to place the cards into one of four categories: Nouns, Pronouns, and Verbs.

A Noun commonly refers to a person or persons, places, or things [examples: girl, boy, dog, home, meadow].

A Pronoun is a word that commonly stands in for an already mentioned noun or as a reference to oneself and other persons [examples: he, she, they, we, I, me, them].

A Verb shows action [example: jump, run, was, has] or an occurrence [examples: is, exists, lives, stay] or state of being [examples: satisfied, rejoice, enjoy].

Each Reading with Ease: An Alternative Method builds on the process of classifying words as parts of speech.

Below are headings to copy to use that provide clues as to the words that belong to each part of speech. It is also helpful to use the www.dictionary.com app or website to assist a learner to identify the part of speech a particular word belongs.

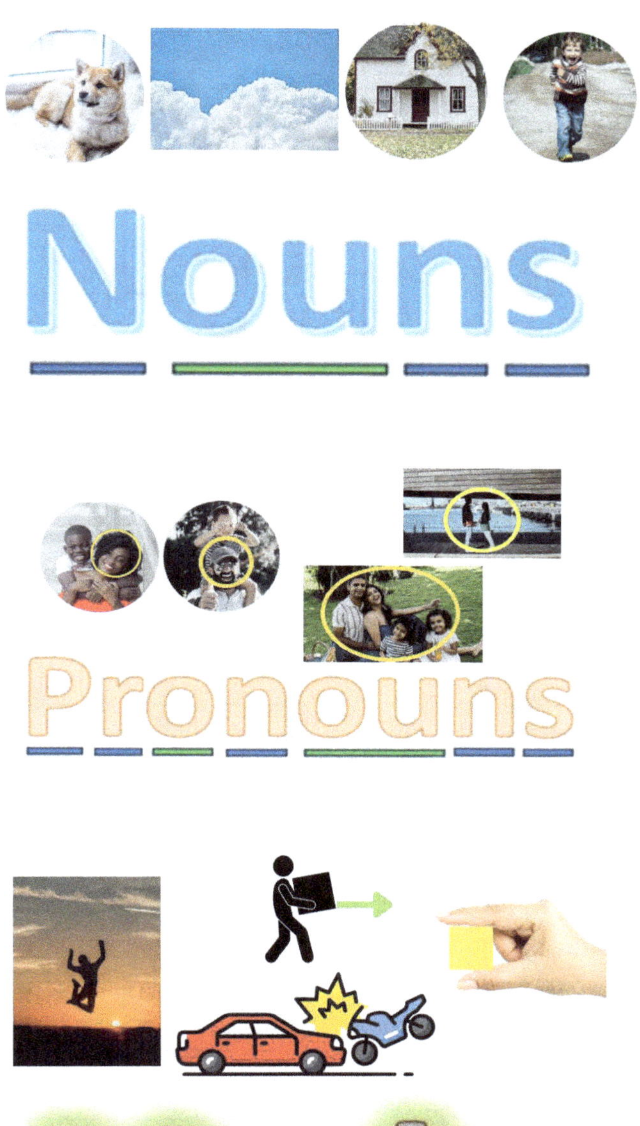

Appendix

Master Word List Data Sheet

(Track progress over time, copy this page often as needed)

Word	Story Number	The Date a Word is Mastered		Word	Story Number	The Date a Word is Mastered
able	9			between	11	
above	8			birds	6	
add	9			birthday	3	
against	17			blanket	16	
air	6			blew	10	
along	4			body	16	
amphibians	6			bowl	1	
animal	2			breathe	6	
animals	6			broke	10	
answer	9			certain	16	
area	17			chameleon	5	
beautiful	5			change	5	
become	15			city	10	
bed	2			close	10	
bedroom	5			color	5	
began	11			complete	16	
begin	11			correct	9	
below	11			country	12	

Master Word List Data Sheet
(Track progress over time, copy this page often as needed)

Word	Story Number	The Date a Word is Mastered		Word	Story Number	The Date a Word is Mastered
covered	16			face	13	
cried	16			fear	13	
dark	13			few	12	
days	2			field	17	
didn't	16			figure	17	
different	2			fish	4	
during	16			floor	4	
early	16			follow	5	
earth	12			form	7	
easy	17			gills	6	
eat	1			goes	2	
end	5			goodbye	2	
enough	12			grains	4	
even	20			group	12	
ever	17			happen	3	
example	12			happened	17	
eye	4			heard	18	
eyes	13			high	13	

Master Word List Data Sheet
(Track progress over time, copy this page often as needed)

Word	Story Number	The Date a Word is Mastered		Word	Story Number	The Date a Word is Mastered
himself	17			late	13	
holding	1			learn	8	
hope	14			leave	14	
hoping	1			left	4	
hours	16			leg	10	
however	12			letter	3	
hundred	18			life	15	
idea	13			line	7	
I'll	17			list	12	
important	9			listen	18	
insect	11			lives	10	
it's	9			living	8	
kindness	1			looked	11	
king	18			low	20	
knew	18			lungs	6	
land	6			mammals	6	
large	5			map	19	
last	13			mark	19	

Master Word List Data Sheet
(Track progress over time, copy this page often as needed)

Word	Story Number	The Date a Word is Mastered
may	1	
means	3	
measure	19	
might	14	
mile	15	
miss	14	
moment	10	
most	7	
mountains	10	
move	4	
music	18	
name	2	
near	10	
need	7	
next	3	
north	19	
notice	20	
numerals	9	

Word	Story Number	The Date a Word is Mastered
numerous	6	
often	14	
order	18	
other	1	
page	3	
paper	3	
party	3	
passed	18	
pattern	20	
pet	5	
piece	20	
place	3	
plan	18	
plant	14	
planting	14	
point	7	
practice	9	
products	20	

Master Word List Data Sheet
(Track progress over time, copy this page often as needed)

Word	Story Number	The Date a Word is Mastered
put	1	
qualities	12	
rabbit	2	
reached	19	
really	14	
remember	20	
ring	4	
same	7	
sand	4	
second	12	
seem	13	
seen	20	
sentence	7	
set	7	
several	20	
shelf	11	
ship	19	
should	7	

Word	Story Number	The Date a Word is Mastered
side	15	
sitting	11	
skill	9	
something	15	
sometimes	13	
sound	7	
south	19	
spell	8	
state	15	
still	2	
stops	19	
story	15	
strange	11	
strong	17	
study	8	
such	8	
sure	20	
tail	5	

Master Word List Data Sheet
(Track progress over time, copy this page often as needed)

Word	Story Number	The Date a Word is Mastered		Word	Story Number	The Date a Word is Mastered
talk	15			years	8	
then	1			young	14	
thing	11					
things	8					
thought	15					
through	8					
told	18					
took	14					
town	19					
travel	19					
turn	9					
watched	4					
week	3					
were	2					
where	1					
wind	10					
without	15					
world	8					

Afterword

YES! There are four (4) more volumes in the planning stage that will complete this first series of Reading with Ease: An Alternative Method. Each supplementary volume will include 200 additional words from Fry's word list. Each word will be paired with representational images as well as phoneme visual breakdowns. And, similar to this volume 3, there will be 20 short stories, each comprised of 10 new words.

May your learner's reading journey be filled with the joy of discovering the wonders of written language!

Kindest regards,

Elaine M. Peters

www.ingramcontent.com/pod-product-compliance
Lightning Source LLC
LaVergne TN
LVHW081149110826
845149LV00008B/1608
* 9 7 8 1 9 6 9 9 7 8 9 6 8 *